PEKINGESE

Mrs. Herminie Warner Hill is Mrs. Lunham of the famous post-war partnership of Lunham and de Pledge, owners of the world-famous "Caversham" Pekes. This partnership ended on the marriage of Mrs. Lunham in October 1955, when the whole of the kennel reverted to Miss de Pledge, including their world-famous Champion Caversham Ku-Ku of Yam for which £10,000 genuinely offered had been refused.

Mrs. Warner Hill has gathered together all her vast knowledge of management, breeding and showing into this book.

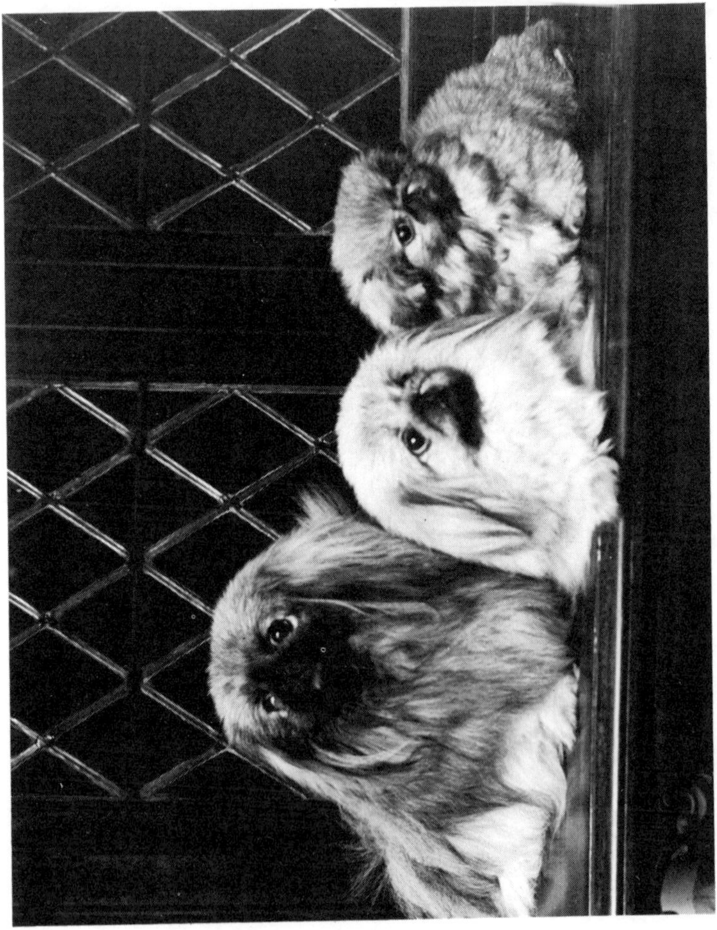

PEKINGESE

BY

HERMINIE WARNER HILL

FOYLES HANDBOOKS
LONDON

ISBN 0 7071 0379 7

*First published 1957
Reprinted 1969
Reprinted 1970
Reprinted 1973
Reprinted 1976*

© *W. & G. Foyle Ltd. 1957*

ACKNOWLEDGEMENTS

Before embarking on this modest work on this our greatest Toy breed, I should like to record help and kindness extended to me during our successful partnership by my very dear friend, Mary de Pledge. In the general script will be found gems culled from the storehouse of her great, and I might almost say, unrivalled knowledge of the breed.

I would also like to thank my husband, Frank Warner Hill, for his journalistic help to me in the layout of this book.

Printed and bound in Great Britain by
REDWOOD BURN LIMITED
Trowbridge & Esher

CONTENTS

CHAPTER		PAGE
1	INTRODUCTION	7
2	HOW TO BUY AN ADULT AND CHOOSE A PUPPY	11
3	KENNELLING	15
4	GROOMING AND HOUSE-TRAINING	18
5	BREEDING	20
6	WHERE WE CAME IN...	30
7	AILMENTS	35
8	AN EYE TO THE SHOW RING	49
9	SHOW ATTENDANCE	65
10	FINAL NOTES FOR ESTABLISHED KENNELS	68
11	PEDIGREES	70
	APPENDIX I—BIBLIOGRAPHY	76
	INDEX	77

1
INTRODUCTION

ENDEAVOURING to create something of general appeal in this short work on the Pekingese, reference will naturally be made to its origin, with reports on the work of some who have spent a lifetime in research. There will be descriptive reference to the general appeal of the Pekingese which has placed it in the unrivalled position as head of the Toy Group of dogs, and also one of the most popular of all breeds, but I am sure you will welcome the inclusion of intimate details on the actual buying of a Peke or the choosing of a puppy, its care and attention during early life, and advice on how to successfully take up the attractive hobby of showing them in open competition.

This latter section will present little difficulty, for I will give you simply and truly my own personal experience of the breed, from a first purchase; the initial win, until the time my growing kennel of Calleva (Roman name of the village in which I lived at that time) Pekes had won over a dozen Challenge Certificates. Also when Miss de Pledge and myself became partners using from thence onward the prefix of Caversham (taken from Caversham Court, home of Miss de Pledge), thus reuniting the Caversham line of Pekingese. It was from the Caversham kennel that I made my first successful purchase. In fact, with but one exception, the whole of the inmates of the Calleva Kennel were of Caversham strain from 1939 onward.

The culmination of this joint effort comes through what has been described—and no valid contradiction has been made—as the greatest Pekingese of all time, Champion

Caversham Ku-Ku of Yam (see Plate II). My own personal biggest winner was Champion Ku-Chi of Caversham for which I paid Miss de Pledge forty guineas when he was eight weeks old. He won for me thirteen Challenge Certificates, and was shown from the Calleva kennel. Transferred to the partnership and back again to the Caversham kennel, he won a further eighteen Challenge Certificates, was twice in the final four contestants for the Best in Show award at successive Crufts Shows and won the supreme award of Best Exhibit in Show at the largest one-day Championship show in the world of those days—the West of England Ladies Kennel Society. All this was accomplished by the time the dog was five years of age. He was then retired from competition, only to meet an untimely death through the dread "smog" always a menace to short nosed breeds.

Already in the kennel was his nine months old son Ku-Ku, who Miss de Pledge and myself had the supreme pleasure of seeing grow on to win *thirty-nine Challenge Certificates under thirty-nine different judges* up to the time of writing, and six times has he won Best Exhibit in Show, All Breeds, at Championship Shows before he was four years of age. Then the fabulous offer was made for him by an agent of an American buyer, one which I may say was increased following its refusal. In this regard I shall have something to say on the export of pedigree stock in a later chapter.

Today the Caversham strain goes on through the numerous winning sons and daughters of this great dog and his offspring, while I rest content, judging and writing about these charming and great little dogs. You may think 'great' a rather peculiar adjective to use about anything so tiny, but believe me they can be as temperamentally great as they are supremely beautiful.

Every dog book gives some theory or other on the origin of this famous breed, but on one thing all are agreed, they were the favourites of the Chinese Court many, many years ago, and in the fortunes, or from the opposite angle, the misfortunes of war, odd specimens fell into the hands of an officer of the invading soldiery and eventually these first examples of the breed reached this country. From such small beginnings did the great family of the modern Pekingese develop. Their great appeal, which obtains to this day, lies in the very gameness of so small an animal. In China they were originally looked on as sporting dogs. They are extremely loyal and extremely good guards, and by their size most suitable for the small establishments of the present time. Add to this their beauty of outline and coat, and their classically developed features, one finds in the Pekingese all that is desirable for a loved companion in the home and a trusted friend and guard of your property.

It has been said with great truth that once a person has owned a Pekingese he seldom changes to another breed, and even should he do so he invariably reverts to his first love. This loyalty to the breed on the part of owners has undoubtedly helped in their great development throughout the years and it is pleasing to record that today unselfseeking owners still concentrate on their further development with little consideration of the financial aspect of their breeding activities. Nonetheless after the initial outlay on foundation stock, you can, with care and good management, make your further breeding efforts and the extension of your kennel, at the very least, maintain itself through your sales of surplus stock, for good Pekingese puppies command a ready sale today, and there is no doubt this will continue in the future.

Good breeding stock, naturally, is expensive, but those with limited means can still set up in an adequate manner through the purchase of a promising puppy from a good kennel, and by exploiting the virtue of patience, eventually commence breeding from a home-reared puppy.

Those who are in a financial position to purchase extensively, with ample house room and staff to care for their dogs can always pay for expert advice, but although my association with the breed comes through a big and well-established kennel, I am writing primarily for the small breeder, though no doubt some of my recounted experiences may be of value to others also.

2
HOW TO BUY AN ADULT AND CHOOSE A PUPPY

When choosing an adult with intention to breed, I would advise you to contact any good kennel and enquire if they have a bitch for disposal from which they have already taken a litter. For one of this type—not a show specimen, but one with no outstanding faults and of good pedigree, the price would be anything from £45 to £75, and where your purse is limited I would sacrifice something in the value of the bitch to obtain one with a good temperament, proved easy whelper and a good mother.

Contrary to what appertains in many breeds of dog, in Pekingese, the good typical bitches run considerably larger than the dogs. The very small types referred to as Sleeve Pekes are not, from their very conformation, a breeding proposition, so choose a bitch, preferably on the big side, rather than one on the small side. They are more likely to give you a larger litter and they are also more easily delivered of their puppies. To give you some definite indication, a young bitch from one to two years old, in good hard condition, can weigh from $8\frac{1}{2}$ - 10 lbs. while the dog should weigh 8 - $8\frac{1}{2}$ lbs. I could go into all the finer points of the brood bitch, but I do not think as an original purchaser, you would be much wiser, and as I said in my opening remarks go to a first-class breeding kennel and place yourself unreservedly in the hands of the proprietor. Do not forget that there is a great reputation at stake, and the genuine breeders are terribly proud of the standing of their kennels.

When you start in the breed is limited by the amount of cash you have to spend, personally I would rather gamble on a good puppy which would cost you from twenty-five to thirty guineas at about three months of age, rather than an inferior adult.

If you have no expert friend to advise you, here again I say, go to the established kennels rather than the pin-money breeder who may know little more than you do about the whole thing. If you are fortunate enough to contact a breeder with a whole litter of puppies for disposal you will undoubtedly be offered your pick, "you pay your money, and you take your choice". In other words, you share with the breeder the ultimate success or failure of the finished adult. Simple indications towards buying a suitable puppy are: do not pick a small one because it happens to be 'cute'. You may be landed with a Sleeve from which you will be unable to breed. Go for a good big bitch. Gently encircle its body with your hands and you will easily feel the large well-sprung ribs so desired. Do not choose one with too short a back. The standard says the Pekingese should have a waist; in fact, a lion-shaped body. Look at the puppy from the front and see if it has a wide chest with good-boned, sturdy legs. Long, straight legs are very undesirable especially if the puppy has no width of chest. A puppy like this can make a very active and gay companion, but I am helping you to choose a breeding proposition with a view to founding a kennel. Naturally, the head is all-important, and the flatter the face the better, but try and avoid a puppy too pinched in the nostril. You may be buying trouble, and this is an actual fault. A beautiful dark, round eye is an essential. I do not mean a pop-eye, but size is essential and expression most desirable. The heads of puppies can change during growth, but there is everything to be said in endeavouring to start right, and a puppy should have over all, a large head, with a flat top-line. By that is meant, as flat as possible between the ears, which while not low set, should not be set right on top of the head. This type, it will be found, later tend to fly their ears, which is another fault. To give you an idea of the correct proportion, width to height, take the shape of an ordinary cigarette packet, and you will get a broad but rather shallow face. There are of course other details such as a broad under-jaw which just fills up the lips. This should never be slack or pendulous. Pekes have a distinct wrinkle up the face and over the bridge of the nose. Some may like this, but I prefer what one may term the 'broken wrinkle', which allows for the nose to come up well between the eyes, and with all these suggestions in mind you should study PLATE VIII which shows a litter of puppies which embodies to the full all the desired requirements, and have since proved themselves on the actual show bench.

If you can visualise in your mind what you want before you visit a kennel so much the better, and you can take your just part of the responsibility in the transaction. Good breeders do not shirk the onus of advising you, but it is more satisfactory if a purchaser has at least some idea regarding what they are buying. In these modern times there is one thing on which I should definitely insist, it is that the puppy should be inoculated with Epivax before leaving the kennel, and in addition to a signed pedigree there should also be a veterinary certificate to the effect that this has been done. Later, of course, you will yourself be dealing with your own puppies, but I strongly recommend that your original puppy should have the treatment in the breeder's kennel where experience in its care ensures that your purchase is sound and healthy on transfer and the correct things have been done to ward off the effects of hard-pad and distemper which caused, in the old days, great mortality among young stock.

Let us suppose your start in Pekes comes through the one bitch puppy, as foundation. You will find if you have been fortunate enough to purchase a good ready-made brood bitch, that she will drop into her appointed place in the scheme of things. Do not let superstition deter you from planning ahead, and do not get muddled ideas about counting chickens, or foolish virgins. You, of course, know the extent of your premises, whether indoor or outdoor kennels will be available, and you will probably be able to decide the ultimate scope of your kennel. My strongest advice here is to keep the extent of your stock well within your own personal capabilities for their care and maintenance. You may later have kennel help, but assistants these days have a habit of vanishing overnight, tempted by the high pay and fixed hours of the factory. A kennel maid must, above all, be an animal lover and not a clock watcher. But more of this anon.

3

KENNELLING

There are many theories on the best way to run a kennel of Pekingese, and here I will give you my views on, not necessarily the perfect way, but, for me, one which has always proved successful.

Pekingese are hardy up to a certain limit—but they have peculiar weaknesses, which, if not guarded against in the way in which one houses these little dogs, can lead to the marring of an adjunct to their great beauty, by this I mean the care of one of their most prized features, the eyes.

Pekingese are susceptible to ulceration of the eye. Sometimes this may arise from a constitutional fault, but more often from the elements such as excessive wind, cold, damp and draughts, or even too much sun. Thus one of the principal features of the housing arrangements should be a well-ventilated but draughtless room or building, kept at an even temperature with suitable platforms or baskets raised from the floor level a matter of a few inches. If, however, one plans to house the dogs in a separate building from the house, one must bear in mind that as a breed Pekingese thrive on human contacts. One can so easily destroy their personality by shutting ten or twelve dogs away where, apart from feeding-time, they scarcely hear a human voice. By nature, Pekingese are brave, gay and intelligent, and these traits of character must be fostered not only in one's show stock, but in the matrons which after all are the backbone of a successful kennel.

No doubt all this, to the modest owner of one bitch puppy, seems to be looking too far ahead, but I am giving you some of the essentials on which you must base your own programme of development. Are your dogs going to be house dogs or kennel dogs, or a mixture of both? Do not forget that a good client will often spring another £10 in purchase price for a house-trained youngster. In any case what applies to a dozen applies equally to your one and only, and in starting off on the right foot you are making things the more easy for the future.

Returning to general kennelling, it must be remembered that Pekingese are great individualists, and as such, each dog should have its own box or basket or sleeping kennel within the room or outbuilding in use. Start quite early in life, for this fosters their spirit of independence, a quality greatly admired.

In the actual sleeping compartment, the dogs should have sufficient space to lie in any position they wish. Any cramping is to be condemned. There are many different views on the bedding to be used. Personally, I have always slept my dogs on blankets in a sufficiently large box for newspaper to be the covering of fifty per cent of the space, thus the dog has the choice of a warm or a cool area in which to sleep, and it will be found that the inmates will alternate in their use according to the general temperature or season.

EXERCISE.

Coupled with kennelling of course, comes the important question of exercise, and from the start it is most essential that one should have some indoor exercising space, however small, available. Regarding general exercise one must be guided by the individual case. As a breed, Pekingese are not constructed (if correctly put together) for long, over-exhausting cross-country running. A Pekingese, given enough freedom, will exercise himself, and at the speed which is correct for his own physical requirements.

There is one golden rule which must be implicitly followed and that is never allow a Pekingese to retire to bed, after exercise, with a damp chest or feet. This can cause many fatal illnesses and also create ulceration of the eyes. An absorbent towel should be on hand at all times in a well-conducted kennel.

4

GROOMING AND HOUSE-TRAINING

I MENTIONED in passing, the higher value of a house-trained Peke when effecting a sale of a pet dog. A Toy dog of any description can be made more valuable and will certainly remove a lot of your worries if it is, in addition, what is known as 'paper-trained'. If you have no covered outdoor exercising run, and only restricted indoor space what a great asset this paper-training can be. This simply means that newspaper can be laid in some inconspicuous corner, and the dog will use it as a private cloakroom in which to answer the calls of nature. We should not hear so many scathing remarks about pet dogs in hotels if they were properly trained to share your bathroom. Training is comparatively simple. When puppies approach weaning time and are being artificially fed, after a feed they immediately proceed to relieve the pressure on their tummies, and for the sake of general cleanliness most kennel people put down for them paper which can be picked up and burnt immediately. It is not a far step, from this early experience, for a puppy to seek the paper put down in the corner, with, in the case of a male, some loose crinkled paper in addition. What a godsend this routine of cleanliness can be to a flat-dweller for instance, or in an hotel, or train when travelling.

In a Pekingese kennel, grooming from an early age is essential and by this I do not mean a hurried flick of a brush. It should be done regularly and thoroughly, and a

GROOMING AND HOUSE-TRAINING

routine evolved for yourself, later to be passed on to your kennel help if you get so far as to need one. Here is the manner in which I have cared for my dogs over the years, from the greatest champions to the 'back-room' girls: otherwise the matrons of the establishment.

Place the dog either on your lap or a table, having with you two bowls of warm water and two small sponges. First, the dog's face and wrinkle should be washed with plain water using one of the sponges, and then it should be well dried. A little boracic powder should then be lightly sprinkled into the wrinkles of the muzzle The ears should be cleaned using dry cotton wool and a little powder—never use water in the ears. I then turn the dog on to its back and sponge, and wash and powder well down the length of the stomach. Then comes the glamorising by means of a brush, and, whatever the cost may be, do get a good one. It should be made of the finest bristle, not nylon or any synthetic bristle, for any harshness may destroy the fine, beautiful fringes. It is in the preservation of this glory in the Peke that I decry the over-use of the comb. If the dog is groomed as I suggest, regularly each day, a knot which needs a comb to remove it should never develop. Growth of tail feathering and ear fringes can be encouraged by special attention, two chief ingredients being time and patience. In this regard if you are tempted eventually to enter the show ring you will find that on the presentation of your dog depends a great part of any success you may achieve.

5

BREEDING

LET us presume you have started operations through the purchase of a good, well-bred puppy from a sound kennel, which of course, as previously suggested, carries a certificate that it has been inoculated with 'Epivax'. Information on its rearing will be found in a special chapter later in the book. After six months of age you must keep watch on the bitch for the advent of her first season. If this should be at six months then I advise that she should be missed, but if her first season should come at nine or ten months, providing she is a well-grown healthy bitch, then you could take a litter from her, and in my own kennel some excellent results have been obtained from an early litter. However, as I am writing for the information of the novice, the best advice is to possess yourself with patience and wait until the second season before commencing breeding operations. You will find generally there are six intervening months between seasons. In the meantime you can be seriously considering your choice of a stud dog, and naturally this is of the greatest importance. In the early days, I do not think I would advise the purchase of a dog. I rather subscribe to the old adage of walking before you start to run. In any case a dog of sufficient merit would be very costly.

I would suggest that you join a specialist club, which means a body of people organised under a President, with Chairman, Secretary and Treasurer and a Committee of breeders whose sole interest is just one breed, and who work for its maintenance in relation to other breeds. In Pekingese, there are four Southern clubs which are registered with the Kennel Club, who, through their standing are allowed to run championship events. A championship event being the highest for competition. These clubs are The Pekingese Club, the oldest and senior club, founded in 1904, which has operated right up to the present time. Hon. Secretary is Lt.-Col. R. V. Bury Perkins, T.D., Lamyatt Lodge, Shepton Mallet, Somerset. Then we have the Pekin Palace Dog Association whose secretary is Mrs. I. V. Driscoll, Ladycross, Keymer, Hassocks, Sussex. There is also the London and Provincial Pekingese Club, Hon. Secretary, Mrs. L. A. Cole, 109 Sunnyhill Road, Streatham, S.W.16; and the Pekingese Reform Association, Hon. Secretary, Mrs. L. K. Howe, 51 Barnfield Wood Road, Beckenham, Kent. The Midlands are served by The Birmingham Pekingese Association, Hon. Secretary, Mrs. B. A. Wort, 94 Elizabeth Road, New Oscott, Sutton Coldfield, and all the foregoing are allowed to promote Championship Events. We also have The British Pekingese Club, Hon. Secretary, Mrs. J. Mitchell, Moorside Farm, Moorlands Road, Birkenshaw, near Bradford; The Invicta Pekingese Club, Hon. Secretary, Mrs. E. N. Adeley, Gaston Gate Cottage, Cranleigh, Surrey; The Ventura Pekingese Club, Hon. Secretary, Miss C. Bennett, Lenhurst, Harrietsham, Kent. Then we have the Scottish Pekingese Association, Hon. Secretary, Miss N. Henderson, Ellenlea, Balmeg Avenue, Giffnock, Renfrewshire, and Northern Ireland is served by The North of Ireland Pekingese Club, Hon. Secretary, Mrs. W. Crowe, 674 Crumlin Road, Belfast; the latter Clubs promoting Members Shows and Open events. Thus you will see that the breed is quite well served by the various organisations. Your first step towards membership is, of course, to write to the Hon. Secretary for details, among which will be found the important one of subscription: generally one guinea per year.

Once enrolled, I would take the first opportunity to attend one of the club shows and meet your fellow members, and there you can look at the winning dogs of that day, to get some idea of an ideal at which to aim. Most winning dogs are placed at public stud, the well-known champions which have proved excellent stock-getters can command a stud fee as high as twenty guineas, while others according to their merit may be used for as little as five guineas. Of course, you can always ask the breeder from whom you purchased the puppy to suggest a stud dog, and he would be willing to help, but on the other hand you might like to choose your own. In this case you should take with you to the show, a copy of your puppy's pedigree and ask any of the leading officials what they would suggest. The breeding of pedigree livestock today is a highly scientific business, and books, nay, libraries have been written on the subject. If you are studiously inclined, buy a book, but if you would rather go on your own fancy when viewing the dogs, by all means do so. A very old breeders' adage is "like begets like" and it is sound in its simplicity to this day. In other words do not go away from the correct type. Had you purchased a proved brood bitch, I would always say go for the very best dog possible regardless of the fee. Apart from anything else it does help if you wish to sell any surplus puppies.

As we are discussing mating a maiden bitch, I would suggest you choose a moderately priced young dog, say brother to or a son of a Champion.

You will realise of course, that after the mating your success or failure lies all with the bitch. Thus in the first place it is of paramount importance that at mating time she should be at the very height of her physical fitness and in good hard and lean condition. A fit, lean bitch when mated, is more likely to give you a large litter of better puppies than one which is over fat. Bloom on a coat is a good indication to health, and if your bitch seems at all dull in coat it would be advisable to dose her for worms before the mating. Actually many breeders do this automatically. This is a simple procedure—any of the proprietary vermifuges will do, and you simply follow the instructions given. Some people will worm a bitch after mating, but it is not really considered advisable, and you could lose the puppies.

Having chosen your dog, written to the owner, and booked a service at an approximate date, you then wait until the time of your puppy's season. A young maiden bitch should be mated fairly early, and you could try her anywhere between the 10th and the 13th days. I strongly advocate that you should take your bitch to the stud yourself. She will be more placid on arrival and your friendly voice will give her confidence, for some youngsters are rather nervy about the first mating. It is not necessary to witness the mating in any reputable kennel for you can be assured the dog you choose will be used, but some ask the owner to be present and even hold the bitch. In any case if you explain to them that you would like to witness a mating by way of education against the time when you own a stud dog, I am sure they will be agreeable. After the mating keep your bitch quiet for twenty-four hours, and keep her segregated until she is quite over her season, when she can return to normal kennel life. If you do not yet possess a safe lock-up kennel and your bitch is a house pet, watch her carefully. Never let her out of your sight when at exercise, and keep her securely fastened up when you are not about, for you will quickly find the local lotharios will be paying you a visit, and you will find they can employ considerable initiative. If you should be unfortunate to have your bitch mismated, get her straight away to a veterinary surgeon— the sooner the better. Once your bitch is free to lead a normal life again, continue with her usual one good meal per day for the next month and then gradually increase her to two meals per day and also offer her milk to drink. In your anxiety to feed the bitch, do not offer any special concentrates, for you do not want to force puppy growth and then have trouble at whelping time.

During this period I advise you to get in touch with a good local veterinary surgeon, one, perhaps, recommended to you as being particularly interested in and good with dogs. I regret that some of the older school interested in horses first and then cattle have only looked on dogs as a lucrative side line, and not kept really up to date. Modern treatments and methods are so far advanced on the times these gentlemen qualified, that one cannot expect them to compete with a younger specialist. Meet him personally, and treat him as you would your family Doctor, a person to appeal to for advice and help in times of stress, and tell him the exact time of the mating of the bitch and he will have the expected birth date in his diary as a possible call.

Actually the bitch should be under your personal care from the fifty-seventh day after mating onwards till she whelps, even to the extent of taking her to your own room. This breed unlike many others who like to be left on their own at this time, at the commencement of labour invariably fly to the one they know best; they like company and help. Show people do not remove any of the long hair, except to free the nipples, but in your case it may, for the first time, be advisable to remove as much hair as is necessary for hygiene and general cleanliness. Assuming the puppies are delivered normally, it is my practice to sever the cord about one inch from the body of the puppy using a simple forceps, and a pair of sterilised scissors. On delivery of the puppy, remove and destroy the placenta as soon as possible and free the puppy's face from the bag or caul in which they are born. If you have the slightest suspicion that all is not well, get on the phone to your friend the vet. immediately. In fact, you may be surprised by a friendly call from him just to see how you are getting along. Of course I have no need to emphasise the necessity for the most scrupulous cleanliness during this time. As soon as possible, without upsetting the new mother, gently sponge her down with warm water where necessary. A plain baby soap is greatly advocated rather than even the mildest disinfectant. You will notice I just said, 'without upsetting the mother', for you will find a complete change in her pre- and post-whelping. The rather nervy little dog seeking your companionship and help, once safely delivered of her puppies and they are actively engaged at the breast, has no time for anyone or anything else, and she should be left perfectly quiet on her own in a shaded room. I do not mean one darkly dismal, but one suggesting tranquility. Just one other great point, you can during whelping, and certainly after whelping, offer the bitch some aired water, but not milk nor milk foods. They can come later, for the bitch can comfortably feed her puppies without any special help, for a surprising length of time, and any rich foods given her would not be really for her own good. She should be kennelled off the floor, with a blanket bed on half of the floor space which need not be very extensive, then a partition a few inches in height to keep the family together when they start to crawl about. On the other half, place newspaper. The bitch can be watered and fed in this chamber, and here you must not expect the young mother to clear up her food at one fell swoop. She will take a mouthful or so, and back she will go, you might almost say, to count her puppies.

Leave her food with her for an hour, then remove it whatever the result; never dish up old or hotted-up leavings, a little, very good and very fresh, is what she needs. A pet bitch about the house is naturally used to having better food than the kennel dogs, and with greater variety. You can very soon get her on to normal diet. Keep an eye on the puppies, certainly, but also keep a very keen eye on the bitch, for through her they survive and she must return to normality in appetite and motions as early as can possibly be achieved. If she looks the slightest bit off colour do not fiddle about and hope for the best. Call in your friend the vet., otherwise it may be too late for him to be of any help. The curse of the medical profession is ailing animals being subject to the ministrations of unqualified people until the moment of extremis arrives, and then the veterinary surgeon is expected to perform a miracle. It can't be done very often, good as they may be, but an early call can ensure almost a certainty. Thus while listening to the devoted lady who knows all about everything and picking out the bits your own intelligence registers as correct, discard firmly all her offers of help and reject firmly her interference. As I have already explained the bitch, after whelping, likes to be alone and the only people who should attend her are those she knows and trusts. What about the stranger vet., you may say. Well, it is a surprising thing that the most distressed little dog, the most nervy and the most suspicious, seem to look on vets. as a very present help in trouble. I cannot explain it, but it is none the less real.

If you are fortunate enough to have the sympathy and interest of anyone of the calibre of Miss de Pledge to consult, and even give you a hand, take advantage of the offer by all means. They very possibly have more experience than a veterinary surgeon in the actual whelping of Pekingese, but with all their knowledge, I am sure if there were complications they would be the first to advise the engaging of professional assistance.

Professional advice is handy in the reinforcing of the bitch's diet in the way of assimilative calcium, etc. This type of thing to be of any use to the puppies must be fed to the bitch in certain forms and only an expert can advise you on the type to be used.

As to the bitch's diet, apart from concentrates, you should give her milk pudding, custard, or egg and milk.

A great standby before myxamatosis cleared off the rabbits, was stewed bunny, shredded; the broth being used to moisten the normal food. Fortunately imported rabbit is still available and is well worth including in the diet. They will take a little shredded raw meat also, and any small portion of green vegetable the bitch will eat; no potatoes of course. If your bitch is a good brood, you will find her very thin after the birth of the puppies. So many Pekes seem to put everything into them which is rather different to other breeds which can whelp down a good nest of puppies and then seem to retain their flesh. However, a Peke will soon pick up body weight, as well as feed the puppies, but may I implore you never to be overanxious about this and overload the bitch's stomach with too much and too rich a diet. Common sense must be used in all things appertaining to the breeding and rearing of highly specialised livestock.

After about four weeks, the bitch can be assisted in her rearing efforts by introducing in very small quantities, artificial food to the pups. Use any of the well-known proprietary brands of special puppy or baby foods, and from now until the puppies are four months old let your watchword be a little and often. Prepare your milk food for the puppies, fresh every meal, and do not be tempted to reoffer any that has been rejected. Keep the pans and feed troughs spotlessly clean with a good scald out every time after use. If you give too rich food to the pups, or too much at a time, you will cause diarrhoea. At the same time you must remember the bitch's natural milk is very rich, cows' milk for instance cannot replace it unless reinforced with some proprietary brand of food. Many breeders keep the odd goat for this reason—goats' milk being that much richer than cows' milk. Puppies seem to thrive on it and even the nursing mother will appreciate a drink now and again.

Most breeders are agreed that at about eight weeks—in other words as soon as the puppies are weaned—they should be treated for worms, and as a vermifuge I recommend a liquid rather than a pill or capsule. These can choke a tiny Peke puppy and are at the best difficult to administer. Liquid vermifuges are in the main of an oily nature, and so in a spoonful of milk you drop your measure of worm medicine and this will be found to slide down the throat comparatively easily.

Just a word of advice regarding this question of weaning. As suggested, the puppies are first taught at four weeks old to lap a little specially prepared milk food, and it can gradually be stiffened with farinaceous powdered food until they are taking something akin to a good porridge. By this time they will also take with advantage a little lightly baked egg custard. While this is going on you can give the puppies a little scraped raw lean beef, starting with a very small portion, little more, say, than the size of a pea and gradually increase until they will be taking beef to the size of a walnut. This should not be solid, remember, but scraped with a spoon from a piece of meat. Scraping is better than mincing, for the small solid piece of minced meat may prove too much for their tender stomachs and small throats.

At seven weeks of age the mother should only visit the puppies to give them one feed per day, preferably in the evening. By eight weeks they can stand alone as a litter and she should not visit them any more.

By this time the bitch herself will be almost dry, for as you artificially feed the puppies you cut down on the bitch's diet, gradually returning her to the normal everyday maintenance amount.

Up to four weeks, your puppies will be with their mother in the nursing part of the kennel on a warm blanket. During this period the dam will act as nanny and keep them clean. With the advent of the artificial diet, which is about the time the puppies begin to crawl about, the partition between his part and the paper lined part can be removed, and you will be surprised how soon puppies will empty themselves in this part of the kennel —an instinctive voluntary act. From this time on, the bitch can be removed in ever-increasing periods during the day time, but returned for the night right up to actual weaning time.

After the actual whelping in the rather shaded quiet room, and about the time when commencement of weaning is considered, the litter may be removed from the box to a basket to enjoy not too strong sunshine out of doors in warm weather; behind glass in cold. Be careful, wherever they may be, that they are free from draughts. Most baby animals can stand a surprising amount of actual cold for their size, but quickly succumb, if subject to damp or draughts.

In the Caversham kennel, no artificial sunshine has been used, but today there are special lamps manufactured which may be suspended over the litter which give forth beneficial rays and a certain amount of warmth. Because we have never used them, do not be put off taking opinion on this question, for many kennels now employ them winter or summer. I may be old fashioned, but for the young, really first-quality balanced diet and natural sunshine with draught-free warmth and cosy bedding, to me are the essentials, although as I say I do not scoff at the artificial aid of modern science.

6

WHERE WE CAME IN

CHEERFULLY optimistic throughout my life, I am taking it that you have arrived at the time when your nest of puppies achieve complete independence from the bitch; have been inoculated with 'Epivax'; are free from worms, and are taking a semi-solid diet backed with scraped raw meat daily. How quickly has the cycle become complete, and any time now you may be entertaining a newcomer to the breed who wishes to buy a puppy. Naturally you will wish to retain the best for yourself, and here you will find the advice of the Stud dog owner invaluable, providing of course you have used one from an established and reputable kennel. You might also find this person your best customer, for the big kennels are always on the lookout for good young stock of their own strain. Get the owner to your house, or being careful the puppies are free from draughts on the journey, you may take the puppies over to the kennel. Supposing you cannot get advice through some cause or other, remember that Pekingese give a good indication of what they will be later in life while still puppies, especially where the head is concerned. Remember, a flat face, large eyes, greater width of skull than depth; then, heavy bone with a short body, and even at an early age, handled delicately, spring of rib will be indicated. With a little observation you will also be able to tell the puppy with the high set tail, by this we mean it is attached to the body at the highest possible point, which helps to create shortness in back, so desired.

In picking your puppy do not be afraid of a bit of size in your bitch, but certainly discard an over-sized dog

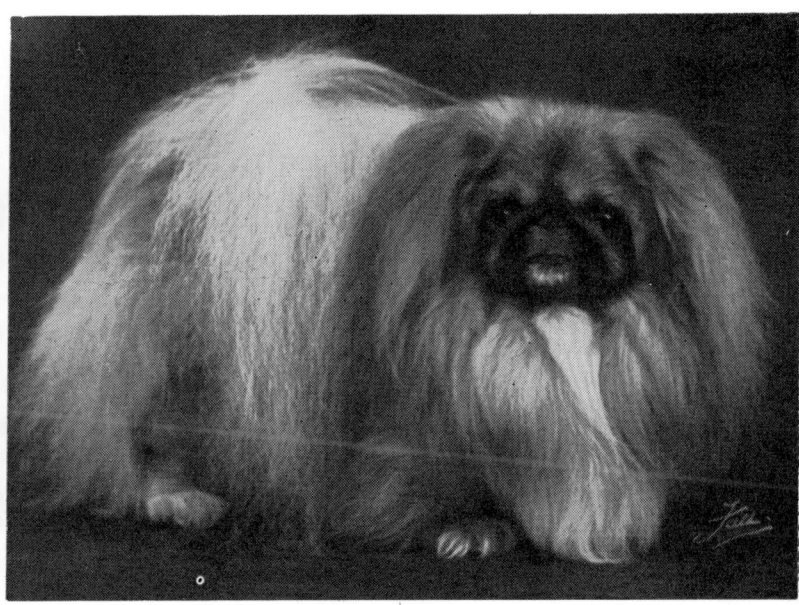

PLATE I. Ch: Ku-Chi of Caversham, owned by Mrs. Lunham and Miss de Pledge.

Photo: T. Fall

PLATE II. Ch: Caversham Ku-Ku of Yam, owned by Miss de Pledge.

Photo: T. Fall

PLATE III.   Ch: Tang-Yua of Alderbourne.   *Photo: T. Fall*

PLATE IV.   Ch: Cheryl of Chintoi.   *Photo: H. F. Pilgrim*

puppy. He may look all right at the time, but size in dogs is a matter of considerable moment. Too big, he cannot win on the show bench, without wins he will not be used sufficiently at stud even to pay for his keep. With bitches it is different, big bitches can be shown and they will win, and they are valued more highly than too small bitches as the matrons of the breed, for the very small bitches should never be mated.

If you are keen on founding a strain of your own and establishing a breeding kennel, in the first instance stick to your bitches and sell your dogs. If you sell a winner or two, so much the better because there will be demand for your next offering. So, first time round I would strongly recommend your keeping only bitches, for your puppy dog cannot be mated to them, and in any case you can once again go to a famous winner and stud dog simply by paying the appropriate fee. You may find eventually, having mated your bitch to a good stud dog, that her daughter will be considerably better than the dam, and thus provide your first step up the ladder. If your original bitch proved a good mother, do not discard her, but mate her again, and for the second generation, I really think I would keep just the one daughter. Later you might dispose of your original bitch, which will always sell as a proved breeder and good mother, but before you even commence breeding operations I can forecast for you the mental stress to be undergone in parting with, after all, your first love. In practice this seldom happens, and when she has given you several litters, the old lady is just kept as the family pet. Unfortunately when only a small kennel can be run, and the Pekes are kept in the house, this question of sentiment can become a menace to the ambitious breeder.

Against the wishes of the kennel owner these individualistic little dogs will annex a place completely their own in the general routine of the establishment and firmly lay claim to a part of the heart and love of their owner. It is inevitable, and this problem has to be met eventually. When kennelled out of doors, and just the odd house pet kept indoors, the problem is more than half solved, for in the first instance the house dog has a major claim on the affections, and he or she will help you to evade the contretemps presented by interlopers trespassing on an established privilege. I know kennels, however, and I must confess in the Caversham kennel, there are too many pensioners kept to be consistent with good business. Business and sentiment, the tycoon would have us believe, do not mix, but who among us is going to make the breeding and selling of Pekingese simply a business? It is far nicer to think that in your breeding activities based on a sincere desire to further the breed interests, that in disposing of your surplus stock you are conveying an actual beneficence on the new owner who in turn will be as appreciative as you have now become, of the charm, the companionship and the great affection one commands in the simple ownership of a Pekingese. Strangely enough you will find as you continue to breed and sell, that a great many men are interested in Pekes and genuinely admire them. In fact, I have seen more men exhibitors in a Peke ring at a Championship show than in a gundog ring, say, Cocker Spaniels. Apart from the aesthetic beauty of the breed it will be found there is a great amount of sportsmanship in their general make-up.

A Pekingese often becomes what you make it, and if you give it the chance to learn and develop its endowed intelligence you will be positively amazed that a dog so beautiful and yet so small can completely satisfy so many facets in our human make-up.

How easy for a breed enthusiast to generalise when our present chapter demands concentration on detail. Let me therefore cast your mind back a few paragraphs when I spoke of the second mating of your established breeding bitch and her maiden daughter. Having proved her with a well-bred dog and she has shown herself to be a prolific breeder and a good mother, you may now go right to the top in choosing a mate for your next litter, and with care you will soon find a champion or a fashionable sire suitable for her. A great recommendation from me is never begrudge an extra pound or two in stud fees to obtain exactly the right dog, and if you can raise the money do not be tempted to offer the stud owner the pick of the litter in lieu of fee, even if this be agreeable. Such a simple transaction in a chancy breeding proposition can lead to endless complications. How would you feel if your bitch only had one puppy, and this you imagine to be a prospective champion, or should she only have two puppies, one a beauty and one a horror, as may happen. You may find yourself cashing up with a lot more money to retain your odd puppy than a plain fee transaction would have cost.

This question of finance affects us all these days, and in my opening remarks I omitted to mention another means you could employ to achieve your heart's desire. Provided you can impress a kennel owner that you are a real dog lover and have a certain amount of common sense, they may entrust to you a bitch on what is known as breeding terms. By this the owner hands over to you a bitch with a proviso that she be mated, when ready, to a dog to be nominated, whether it be in the kennel or belonging to someone else, in which case you may be expected to pay the stud fee.

For keeping and whelping the bitch it may be agreed between you that you share the litter. Of course, in each individual case the details may differ, but that is the overall arrangement regarding a bitch on breeding terms, with the added possibility that following, say two litters, the bitch herself may become your own property. Between people of good intent there is nothing of great moment in an arrangement of this sort, but such is human nature that I urge you to have a formal agreement drawn up stating clearly the demands of the bitch owner and what part you have to play. One dog magazine, published weekly, supplies a form of agreement based on a wide experience in this sort of transaction and a copy will cost you very little. However well you may know, or whatever the standing of the owner of the bitch, I do implore you to have a clear and formal agreement. This is a form of partnership. Although I am not giving you all the snags which may arise, they are none the less there, but may be hidden. The very fact that each side approves this formal agreement seems to prevent, on its own, any untoward happening, and I have known many kennels successfully founded by this means, and lifelong friendships established.

7

AILMENTS

Up to now everything in the kennel and in our breeding activities has gone swimmingly, and of course you may be one of the lucky people who always seem to keep their dogs free from troubles. Because I acquired a house with some excellent indoor grape vines and had initial success in growing grapes, I took a more detailed interest in them and found they could suffer from about fifty kinds of disease, parasitic and otherwise, and without in any way wanting to alarm you, if you pick up a book on dog ailments you will find they can have hundreds of diseases. Just as I did with my grapes I ignored the frightening numbers and concentrated on preventatives and simple treatments and got splendid results. I am going to give you instructions on the more prevalent troubles Pekingese are heir to, and some simple precautions and remedies. Even though a veterinary surgeon earns his living by treating animals, he does not like to be for ever on one's doorstep, called in for very little reason. There will therefore be no resentment in my writing this chapter, nor you in following out my suggestions.

First let me save you a lot of trouble and heartache where a puppy born with a cleft palate is concerned. In practice it has been found that artificial feeding in hopes of a recovery is not practicable, and the best advice one can give is to have them put to sleep immediately this state is discovered. As soon as puppies are born, gently open the mouth and you can soon see that the cleavage in the palate may be small or large, but take my advice and put it down straight away. I regret to say that cleft palate is rather prevalent in Pekes, and seems to come in phases according to the stud dog fashionably in use at the moment.

The most vulnerable part of a Pekingese is of course the large and somewhat protruberant eye, and a complaint you are bound to come across is that of ingrowing eye lashes. As soon as this becomes apparent in a youngster, you should gently turn the lashes back smearing them with a little vaseline to assist in keeping them in place. That great authority Dr. Vlasto, even suggests using a little of the old-fashioned moustache wax the men used when spiky moustaches were fashionable. If this is not successful I would take a pair of small tweezers and pluck out the offending lashes. If you do not take immediate steps to remedy the defect on the lines suggested, the eye will turn blue and become ulcerated, and you may find you will be off to the veterinary surgeon for an operation. Neglect can result in a permanently damaged eye or even its complete loss. Winking and watering are the signs first to be seen from the ingrowing eyelash and do not neglect the warning. Puppies are sometimes born with an extra claw, known as a dew claw, which appears on the inside of the hind leg, slightly above the foot. These are useless appendages and should be clipped off with a pair of sterilized scissors as soon as possible after birth; a very simple and not at all hurtful procedure. The very small wound may be dabbed with Friars Balsam which will stop bleeding and assist in healing. No Peke kennel should be without a bottle of the Balsam in the medical chest, for it can be used on minor wounds, and I personally prefer it to iodine.

There are about a dozen and one kinds of worm, but as far as puppies are concerned they are generally affected with what we look upon as the simple round worm. I have already told you how to administer a dose of vermifuge. Puppies with worms often have great appetites, but do not thrive, and their coats are staring and lack lustre. These are sure signs, so treat them immediately. If unsuccessful in obtaining results, get qualified advice, for there may be some other and more difficult type of worm to treat and of course in the first place, to be diagnosed.

Puppies can develop hernia. A rupture of the groin in a dog should not be neglected. Get some good treatment at an early stage. A simple navel rupture caused very often by a too enthusiastic nursing mother, will sometimes disappear on its own, but if one is seen, be careful to pick up the puppy correctly until the muscles strengthen and it disappears. You will no doubt know how to pick up a rabbit, and the puppy should be supported with a hand under the rump. I do not suggest grasping the ears, but gently clasp round the shoulders.

Just as I said, dogs can have a hundred and one diseases or afflictions. There are two hundred and one cures for them today, and I can only tell you the very best results have been obtained in the treatment of the eye in puppies or adults by using 'Collosal Argentum (Opthalmic)', a Parke Davis product.

I have returned to instruction on the eye, for we were only discussing puppy infection through ingrowing lashes. Eyes can be damaged through cold and draughts, excessive sun or wind, or internal trouble which we refer to in kennel parlance as 'a stomach' eye. On the very first appearances of a blue cast in the eye, use a drop of the Argentum liquid, and repeat every four hours.

At the same time I would give a tablet of cascara, first because the eye infection may be caused through a stomach upset, and cascara is easily administered. Second, this is one of the laxatives that seems to suit this small breed.

On the principal that prevention is better than cure, a simple kennel drill could be the irrigation of the eye with weak Optrex daily when grooming, or use weak boracic water. Here let me emphasise again the need for the utmost cleanliness. You can use warm water to ensure the dissolving of the boracic powder, and a famous matron in a leading nursing organisation told me to use a small jug which had been scalded out and left to cool, in which to prepare the mixture which should be quite weak. When completely cool, pour the liquid into the eye. This is preferable to bathing the eye with cotton wool, for you may by this means introduce a minute particle of wool into the eye which would aggravate any irritation there, or provoke it.

Treatment of animals at all times should be conducted at the very highest level that could be employed in the treatment of a baby.

In this regard, while on the subject of infections of the eye, an exceedingly fine remedy for a number of complaints is Yellow Oxide of Mercury ointment. This can be purchased, should I say 'commercially', in the usual chemist type of box, quite cheaply, but here again comes danger in administering it. I would suggest you purchase it in tube form, with an administering nozzle with protective sealing cap. Thus you administer it in completely pure form, free from accumulating dust.

A very small amount squeezed on to the ball of the eye will cause the dog to close it, and then very, very, gently massage the eye THROUGH the lid. Superfluous ointment will come from the eye on to the lids, and will tend to clear any outside encrustation. In this treatment, little, lightly and gently are the three watchwords.

By this time your enthusiasm to become a Peke owner may be beginning to wane, and you may even decide against owning or breeding them altogether. So let me tell you that although grapes can develop a hundred diseases, parasitic and otherwise, I still grow them, and have found over a long period a vine never gets the lot together, and you will find that your Pekes in the common law of averages never develop all the troubles to which I am referring, at the same time. In fact you can go for years without anything but the most minor, and simply dealt with, complaints developing. In common parlance, because I am telling you of things WHICH CAN HAPPEN—*I do not mean they will happen. Fore-warned is fore-armed, and if you live miles from a decent vet. you may be glad I have included this lengthy chapter in my book, if one or another of these sometimes disturbing things arise.*

The modern development in dog foods has been so extremely good that two dreaded maladies have practically been cleared. I refer to canine hysteria and rickets, which strangely enough, in the old days, were, unknown at the time, so very closely allied because the condition was brought about by bad feeding—insufficient or the wrong type of food.

Hysteria you would have said was a mental disorder, which of course it is, BUT it is induced by incorrect feeding. In the pre-war days when it was not uncommon for twenty show dogs to go off into fits together at a show, many people said it was caused through ear canker, or a small worm lodged in the ear. It was imitative. One dog would start with wild yelping with staring eyes, and if it could slip its lead would chase in wild circles, until completely exhausted it would dive into some dark corner, a pitiable cringing object. A dozen others predisposed to the malady would imitate until pandemonium reigned. The terrier men, or some of them, to be correct, would smartly smack the faces of their charges and dump them in the dark of their travelling box. Actually my husband, Frank Warner Hill, a great gundog breeder of the between war years, was one of the first to realise the cause, and developed a cure of the only case which happened in his kennel, which was serious enough, for nine seven-month-old puppies and their dam were all involved. He cured them and then set about thinking on the lines of cause and effect. He wrote a paper on his findings which was sent to some authority in London by Mr. Lloyd, a famous veterinary surgeon in those days. The paper was entitled '*A Layman's Theory on Canine Hysteria*'. He, as he says, received 'quite a number of medals' for his work. It is rather interesting to follow his simple reasoning which up to that time had never occurred to anyone else. He thought of the hearty eater, who enjoyed huge meals without any ill effect, who disturbed by news, perhaps war news, or some tragedy closely affecting himself, who instead of enjoying his food would prop a newspaper up in front of himself at table; reading as he ate; probably worrying, and within a short time developing severe indigestion. The stomach adversely affected by the mind.

In reverse, could not an upset stomach affect the mind equally? From then on it was but a short step to establishing that the idea was correct. He knocked off all biscuit foods, or any bread, put the dog on a light diet—fish, tripe, etc., and then, being a corn miller, he stone-ground some good English wheat, dressed out the rougher offal, and baked unleavened bread with the pure wheat meal. This and raw meat became the dogs' staple diet with occasionally cooked meat and this home-made bread scalded down with meat gravy. The kennel was finished for ever with hysteria. Quite unknown, and no way in collusion, a gundog and Dalmatian breeder, Mr. Frank Swann of Cromford, commenced working on similar lines, and so not long afterwards my husband got some outside confirmation. By experiment it was found dogs could be thrown into canine hysteria and brought out of it simply by diet. Unqualified, neither could say what it was about the flour of which the bread and biscuit were made, which created the hysteria. Almost twenty years later, and it took him a long, long time and many experiments on animals, dogs in particular, an eminent veterinary surgeon was to surprise us all by writing a leader in the *Lancet* on canine hysteria, its cause and cure. He was Professor Mellanby, and he it was who actually discovered the active agent in creating canine hysteria. It was created in the manufacture of flour, in its bleaching or other processes, and it was called Agene. What common sense had achieved so many years previously, scientific research proved conclusively. Thus our dog food manufacturers were able to provide us with many "hysteria free" foods, and it is many years now since I have seen a dog affected by canine hysteria. In fact, today many newcomers to dogs do not even know what we mean and they have never seen a case. The lesson to be learned of course is in all cases where dogs are concerned and you are uncertain on what line to take, use your common sense. All the modern well-known dog foods are safe and very good value, expensive though they may be when compared with pre-war prices. I have actually visited factories, and dog's biscuits are made today under precisely similar conditions as biscuits for human consumption. In fact, I would not have the slightest hesitation, if hungry and nothing else was available, in eating dog biscuits. Actually I have done so when returning from a show on a non-diner train, hours late through breakdown.

Turning to rickets, which of course will never be completely abolished, we find they are caused through bad feeding. A blown out dog crammed full of what the kennel folk call "fill belly", meaning quantity with very little nutriment, cannot grow sound, good quality bone. You will find the joints will swell, the legs become deformed, and if treatment is not given a dog can soon develop into a permanent cripple. It is much better to give your dog good food and leave him a little hungry than give him food of twice the bulk with only the same nutriment. Pekes of course are not all that expensive to feed, but my remarks apply just the same to a kennel of Great Danes.

A good varied diet which has already been indicated is the first consideration, and you may, while growth takes place, give your dog a teaspoonful of cod liver oil every day and the colloidal form of Parish's Chemical Food, about fifty-fifty mixture. I advise the colloidal form, because the dog is able to assimilate the food better in this form.

Bad kennelling can also aggravate rickets, but I don't suppose you will be guilty of that. Dogs can stand cold, but not damp or draughts, so set your kennels out accordingly. Lack of exercise can be a contributing factor also, but unlike some breeds such as Greyhounds, which require extensive walking. Pekes will exercise themselves in quite a small paddock. They will give themselves sufficient exercise, and what is more, at the speed most suited to them. From their very conformation Pekes are slow moving animals, and if you do take one for a walk, let it be a leisurely one, and if you have to quicken up through rain or time, pick the dog up and carry it. I hate to see people dragging their dogs along by the neck, and feel tempted to mete out similar treatment to them. Even dog judges are not guiltless. My own dogs have been subject to such ridiculous demands that had they not been modified I should simply have removed the dog from the ring. A Peke has a slow, dignified rolling gait in front, with a quick, close scissored action behind, and remember once again *he was not built for speed*. If Pekes are too slow for you—then go in for a Whippet.

To sum up the position, my suggestion is to feed the best of foods, coupled with the simple additions I suggest. There are many new products offering you all the vit mins conducive to good growth, but in my opinion concentrated or synthetic administration of vitamins cannot in ang way compensate for lack of proper nourishment.

In the old days in Sheffield, a great cutlery centre, in the small back-to-back tenement houses, there were many

AILMENTS

cases of rickets, in the days when a baby was weaned by a potato chip bought from the local fish and chip shop, dipped into beer, and offered in the form of a dummy tit. Those were the days when staghorn was good enough for the workers, and ivory handles for the upper ten. In the production of these handles, when grinding and buffing the ivory to shape, there was produced what was termed ivory dust. In cases of rickets in children, certain old doctors always told the parents to get some of this highly volatile ivory dust, scale it, and feed it to the infant in the form of jelly. My husband has used this food with great success for his gundogs in the post-war era. I realise it is difficult to find a cutler's shop where ivory dust can be obtained, but should you find a source of supply, I suggest you use this in preference to most of the proprietary brands of anti-ricket and bone-forming productions. Strangely enough in the old days, instead of being marketed to the best advantage, it was used mostly in the manufacture of lamp black. Years ago at Sheffield University an eminent professor discovered how to embody the essential vitamins in an acceptable form, and thus was born the numerous malt extracts. One of the first was radio malt and it was very effective. Today, concentration has resulted in the capsule and the phial, such as Alibrol, Radiostoleum, etc., all of which contain an enormous vitamin content. However, where dogs are concerned you should look on these things as a very present help in trouble, when your normal diet chart seems to be lacking in something essential.

Dogs for all our warping of their characters and physique are still very near to nature, in fact there is one very active school who scorn all the products of modern science and only use and recommend nature's own helps and remedies in the form of herbs. Their followers are just as bigoted as their opponents, but there is nothing to stop you using the best of two worlds, though I would remind you that dogs are carnivorous and not herbaceous animals. The cow which depends on grass for life has only one set of teeth in the lower jaw, the dog has a very good full mouth of teeth with strong incisors. You would not feed meat to a cow, therefore do not feed grass to a dog except in the way of variation in diet. Meat, raw or lightly cooked is the dog's natural diet. Back it up by all means with properly produced wheat products, but always keep the balance in favour of meat.

Even in these difficult times there is available in fair quantity, sheep's paunches, and there is nothing better for a dog, cooked or raw.

The main crop of puppies come in the spring, and a sheep or lamb killed at this time has a stomach full of spring grass. Buy the paunches just rough cleaned, and try pegging one down on a lawn for the puppies to pull and tear at. They can tear bits off and eat them and thus get a completely natural animal and vegetable diet. Stewed tripe is a famous and very nourishing dish and you can stew your paunches and thicken with wheatmeal or scalded dog biscuit.

Because of cheapness I have known people give dogs and puppies low grade or skimmed milk. This is quite wrong, for this is pig food.

Even the best full cream milk, when offered to puppies, should be augmented with additional dried milk-powder or any of the advertised milk products. Which you prefer does not matter, that you use them is the important thing. By doing so you give smaller quantities which have a richer quality. Do not think I am over-emphasising this point, for it is important. To raise strong, healthy young stock, feed the very best you can provide, in rich, fully balanced strength, and sacrifice quantity in its favour. To get a stomach-distended, rickety animal, offer quantity

AILMENTS

instead of quality. Rather than do this get rid of the dog for you are doomed to failure anyway.

Coupled with incorrect feeding comes skin trouble. Bad feeding can create one kind and foster others. In dealing with skin trouble from a parasitic origin let me commend to you one of the oldest firms in this country. Famous in the olden days for their Sheep Dip, Messrs. Cooper, McDougal and Robertson, with the progress of modern science, decided to extend their preparations to include special treatment confined purely to dogs. Among their now many products the two of greatest use to a kennel owner are 'Pulvex', a dry powder, and 'Kurmange', a wet dressing. Well-kept dogs should keep clear, but accidents can happen and I commend to you one or the other of these products. If perchance any dog develops something which is beyond ordinary powers of diagnosis, then write to the firm for advice. Unless completely sure, they will send you back to your old friend the veterinary surgeon, who in turn may still recommend later, once the trouble is diagnosed, one of Cooper's famous products. While on the subject of proprietary medicines, one of the most famous and the oldest is that rather forbidding, and certainly smelly product, Benbows Dog Mixture. I once was given instruction how to make it, but I can tell you it is much better to pay your money for the finished product, and in any case there may have been something added to the usual blending of Linseed Oil and Sulphur. Do not be frightened when the only thing they proudly tell you is that it has been given to every Greyhound who has won the Waterloo Cup. It is good for small dogs too, and in addition to a nerval conditioner, a dog given Benbows regularly is practically immune to worms.

For those who like a powder form of conditioner there is another world-famous and esteemed remedy—Bob Martin's condition powders, and of much later origin, the Karswood Dog Powders. Both are good, safe, and easily administered by the novice dog owner, and being safe within very wide margins of the recommended dose, there is no danger of any overdosing.

I suggested earlier that dogs could get one hundred and one things wrong with them and for which there were two hundred and one remedies, but if you care for your dog, do not neglect the simple rules of health and kennel hygiene. There is nothing to be afraid of and nothing of moment which these tried and true old remedies and preventions cannot cope with.

At this moment let me give you some very good advice. If a dog is off colour, never panic. Conquer your natural distress and bear on the problem a little common sense.

Even old dogs can look like death one evening and be galloping about the room next morning. Puppies are even worse. I have in my youth, before I learned these facts and after sitting up three nights with some ailing puppies, had to go to bed eventually completely exhausted, heartbroken and dispirited, only to come down next morning to see the expected corpses sitting up and looking round for food.

Here I might say that it is quite surprising the length of time a dog or puppy can go without food without any great inconvenience. They may drop in condition, in fact some breeds seem to go down like a pricked bladder, but when over their indisposition they regain form just as quickly. Sickly or well, only offer your dogs food, never leave it available for them. It simply goes sour and unpalatable. If you are worried about them not eating, then you can give your invalids English honey and water. It keeps them in condition and seems to be easily assimilated. There is in this country a famous kennel of Setters whose owners attribute the low mortality during an attack of the devastating hard-pad to giving them honey and water. Another great kennel of cockers buys honey by

PLATE V. Ch: Ku-Jin of Caversham. *Photo: T. Fall*

PLATE VI. Ch: Kyratown Lu Tong of Redstock. *Photo: Dewhurst*

PLATE VII.   Chs: Shama and Ku-Chi of Caversham   *Photo: T. Fall*
and their winning litter.

PLATE VIII.   Ch: Ku-Jin of Caversham and his litter   *Photo: H. F. Pilgrim*

the hundredweight and gives it freely to rearing puppies and to adults when conditioning them for show.

Doggy ailments are often accompanied by extreme looseness of the bowels. White of egg cut up with a knife and fork—do not laugh—you can actually cut up stringy white of egg by this means, can be mixed with water and administered spoonful by spoonful. Another tip, and this time applied to Pekingese in my own experience; in cases of a gastric condition, take all normal drink away and offer the puppy or dog, flat soda water. Very simple but it seems to work.

For our small dogs—rather expensive in the case of big ones I admit—I thoroughly recommend the products of 'Brands', particularly their essence of beef and of chicken.

Actually I know a principal of this great firm and can testify to the supreme excellence of their products. These essences seem to be acceptable to a sickly dog or puppy, and they seem to keep this highly concentrated food in their stomachs without the sickness more bulky foods seem to bring on. Just because the dog keeps down the small amount given and seems to rally, do not on any account increase the dose, otherwise you will have a stomach full of concentrated food and defeat your object. As the dog picks-up, rather decrease the essence and give more normal food, or a mixture of both until normal appetite and assimilation is achieved. It is a fact that more dogs are ultimately killed by overfeeding than underfeeding. If you overfeed your Peke I can promise you its life will be cut by one third of its normal span.

A fat dog becomes asthmatical, irritable in temperament and gross to look at, addicted to skin trouble and other affections. Use common sense at all times—it comes before the most well-informed or learned tomes on development, deterioration or maintenance; it is cheap and effective, and is a good stand by until qualified help and advice can be obtained. You will appreciate throughout this little book that I have particularly emphasised that I am giving you my version of what to do and how to do it. In minor matters I believe I am correct, in major matters I KNOW I am correct in advising qualified advice.

8

AN EYE TO THE SHOW RING

THE first essential in showing a dog is that it should be registered with the Kennel Club at No. 1 Clarges Street, Piccadilly, London, W.1. If you have bred a litter, we take it that your bitch is already registered and you have used a registered dog. Since the war the scale of charges has altered considerably but at the moment the charge for the registration of a puppy is 5/-. Write to the Kennel Club who will supply you with a form of application for registration. If your bitch has only part of a pedigree and is unregistered, or if the dog is unregistered, by paying a fee and obtaining a certificate from a Championship Show judge of the breed—often recommended by the Kennel Club—you can obtain a certificate. This should be done for reasons of economy in registration of a litter of puppies and also for the good of the stud book.

Let us take it that the papers of both sire and dam are in order, and thus you will have no trouble in registering the puppies if you wish to apply for your own prefix. You will have to submit the name required, and the choice of several other names if this one is not available. You must not use the name of a town or county, nor a family name. The Kennel Club like a built-up name of no particular identity as a prefix and on payment of so much per year or compounding for a lump sum, becomes your own property. My own registered prefix is Calleva (Roman name for Silchester where I lived, but I doubt if the modern name would have been approved). Miss de Pledge owns the prefix of Caversham—she previously lived at Caversham Court. If you are breeding extensively, the ownership of a prefix becomes a 'trade mark' for the products of your kennel. Every dog and every puppy you register as in the case of Miss de Pledge—Caversham Billie, Caversham Jimmie, and so on, will hold the original prefix throughout life, only one addition to the name can be made, but not an alteration.

Just to give you an idea what I mean by applying for a 'built-up prefix', say for instance your name is Carter. You could apply for the prefix of Recart, and if it is granted call your dogs Recart Robert, Recart Royal, etc., they sound well and they keep your name to the fore, for people will soon realise the significance of the prefix.

With the exception of Litter classes, where you show your babies from the nest, a puppy cannot normally be shown until it reaches the age of six-months. As this book has been written for the smaller novice breeder, let us presume you followed my original suggestion, now have a puppy six months of age, and have already had it registered with the Kennel Club.

There are all sorts of ways you can set about showing it. You can join a local canine society many of which have what are termed 'Monthly Match Nights'. These are by way of being social events, and a learning ground for young judges. Novice exhibitors like yourself can obtain ring practice with your dog at the minimum of expense. Apart from your original small fee of membership there are no charges in competing at matches. Here you are simply showing your puppy against another one of the same breed or perhaps of a different breed, and the judge decides which is the better of the two. A night or two at 'the matches' and you will feel quite at home, for members will be pleased to help and advise you. Your puppy will also be acclimatised to the bustle of a show ring and have gained confidence. The next step is that you can enter for your local club's member's show. These are held periodically and are much more serious in competition; in fact, today many member's shows reach a very high level in competition.

The average charge per class at a member's sanction show is 2/6. At all dog shows it is a Kennel Club rule that the first prize must be four times the entry fee, thus if you pay 2/6 per class at a Members' show, you compete for a 10/- first. You may find there is no special class for your Pekingese, so just enter it in the puppy class open to all breeds, and see what happens. If, however, you have taken advice before the show and someone with knowledge has told you the puppy is a good one, you could enter several more lower classes, such as maiden and novice classes. The secretary or other of the officials will be glad to advise you.

If you win, do not be too elated and if you lose do not be too down-hearted. You must not be satisfied until you have entered your Peke at an Open or a Championship show, where there are special classes for the breed and a fully qualified Pekingese judge. Here you will meet lots of fellow exhibitors. Listen to what they say, and after judging you can have a quiet word with the judge. Explain that you are a novice, and ask his private opinion of your dog, and whether it is worth further showing.

There is a lot more to dog showing than simply winning a prize with your dog. There is anticipation and excitement, and one can take great pleasure in meeting so many people interested in dogs and your breed in particular.

The very words 'dog show' should give you a clue regarding your own dog. You must make the best of it in every way possible, for in a close decision very small points can sway the judges' decision in your favour. To look its best a Pekingese, or any other dog for that matter, must be in good health and condition and all long-coated breeds must be in full coat. Do not waste your money showing a Pekingese before his coat is fully grown, though of course allowance may be made for a puppy exhibit.

Taking it that your youngster is fit, sound and in good coat, let me give you some hints on training for the show. In the first place you must train him to walk freely on a light cord show lead, without having to be dragged along. Persevere with him until he will walk quite happily alongside you; will stand when you do, and will look up at you when you speak to him. During this period, if yours is a purely women's establishment, get some men to talk to the dog, give him tit-bits to eat, and by any means you can think of get him to approach men with confidence and be handled by them, for although a toy breed, they are often judged by men. In your exercising, you must get the dog used to crowds and noise. A good training ground is a station platform. Pay your penny and mix with the crowds of passengers. Gradually the dog will become used to the bustle; the feet of strangers almost treading on him, and the alarms attendant on a train leaving a platform. Once he has gained his confidence in a place like this you can be pretty sure he will not be frightened by dog-show crowds, the dangers of feet in a crowded ring and the handling by a complete stranger. He will go into a ring with his tail carried firmly over his back. This he must do. A Peke which will not carry his tail, however good he may be from other show points, cannot win, and so I do strongly say to you, get the dog over any nervous tendencies before you even enter for a show. Match nights can of course be looked on as training grounds also, for the results are not officially recorded and you will find other people using this method of novice showing as a training ground for their young stock. As to the actual type of lead to use, I advocate a collar and lead rather than the slip-over lead. Buy the thinnest rolled leather collar you can find of the correct size. Fasten it round his neck over the mane. Then gently lift the mane over the collar until it is next to his skin, and when settled there it should be just finger tight, in other words you can just slip your finger round the dog's neck between it and the collar. Then attach to the collar a swivel, light cord lead, making the attachment under the dog's chin, so that if you have properly trained your dog he appears to be walking at your side without a lead at all. The lead loops slightly from under his chin and is quite slack. You can give the dog, when necessary, an encouraging tug or slight jerk, but never drag on the lead until the point of attachment comes on top of his neck. It is unsightly and also handicaps the dog.

Let us presume you have gone through all these exercises at home and your dog is reasonably amenable to lead control. You have entered him for a show, you have your admission ticket and away you go. Be in good time, for the order of judging through unforeseen circumstances may be altered and you may be in the first class instead of say the sixth. You cannot just rush to the show, go straight in the ring, and expect to win. The final touches should be done at the show, and time given for a novice exhibit to settle down and gain full composure.

Very often the exhibitor's number is given out in the ring by a steward, so if you have not got yours, do not start fussing and plaguing everyone. Look at the other exhibitors and see what they are doing. If, of course, they have their numbers, then go to the secretary and explain yours has not been delivered, and the matter will be put right.

Have your dog nicely groomed, and nicely composed, and when your class number is called, simply walk into the ring with the dog under your arm and keep him there. Do not crowd round the table snatching at number cards, the steward will find you and hand you your number, and here let me say, have some means ready of attaching it to your person in the region of the heart. You can buy a safety-pin, or a special gadget at the shows in the form of a clip. Nothing is more maddening to stewards, judges and ringsiders if your number is not readily to be seen. Spectators want to know which dog is which, and your exhibited number is their only means of identification. Pekingese are judged rather differently to other breeds. A specialist judge seldom asks you to walk round the ring in a circle, though perhaps a variety judge will ask you to do so. In this case have the lead in your left hand and walk in the line in an anti-clockwise motion.

Let us take it that you are showing under a specialist. In nine cases out of ten the judge will ask you to walk your dog before it is handled. You will be called from the line up to the judge, who will tell you to walk your dog, so put it on the floor and if necessary touch up his tail over his back with your brush. Then walk slowly down the ring, turn round and come back again. Do not rush the dog; do not get excited; just keep calm and let your dog walk at your side as he has been trained. Strangely enough the best trained dog at home will seemingly, for very devilment, misbehave when in the ring. Here only experience can come to your aid. A touch of the brush, a jerk on the lead, or any other reasonable means you can devise, may have to be used to get the dog showing his paces correctly. If your dog has moved nicely, on arrival back to the judge, pick the dog up and offer it to him for examination. Many will take it from you, look at it, then give it back to you and motion it to a table in the ring where the judge will again examine it. One by one the other exhibits are treated alike until there is a full row of Pekes on the table with the handlers standing behind them. The dog's manes are lifted up; their feathering touched up with a brush and the dog will look its very best. After examination the judge might ask for, say, five to be brought from the table, then you immediately put your dog on the floor, adjust his coat if necessary, and let him stand on a slack lead while you attract his attention

AN EYE TO THE SHOW RING

and keep him showing and attentive. By this time you know you are well on the way to winning a prize. You may be asked to move the dog again, or perhaps not, but eventually the judge will motion to one of the exhibitors and the first so nominated goes automatically to the head of the table, and the others take up position in order as they are called.

Now is the time to have your dog looking its very best; its mane just right and its ear furnishings giving all the appearance of breadth and flatness of skull you can achieve. The judge then makes a final decision and, wishing to change the placings will tap the table in front of one dog owner and then tap the table at a higher or lower position as the case may be. The other owners will then move up and separate to make room for you. Just imagine you are standing third from the top of the table, there is a tap for you and you move up one, another exciting moment or two, and then a final motion and you are at the top and have won. Most judges will then order the first four dogs again to the ground in the same order in which they were finally placed on the table. The judging book will be marked, and until this is done you have not won, so never slack off showing until you see it happen. Then the stewards will call out the numbers of the exhibits as they are given their prize cards. The first time this happens to you, you will not walk out of the ring, you will float out in a happy daze, as proud and pleased as if you had just won the huge cup for the best of all breeds at Crufts.

Now as this is a fairly big show, there may be, say, eight classes for Pekes, and you may have entered only one or two of them. Presuming you win them, you naturally stand as an unbeaten dog. Do not rest on your laurels, for there is more to come. Keep an eye on the judging and the ring while your dog is resting in its box. Presently you will hear the cry "All unbeaten dogs and bitches in the ring please". This means the judge is going to pick the best dog, the best bitch and then finally the best of breed. Do not get excited (if you can help it); enter the ring with the others and stand quietly awaiting the judges approach or instruction. You will perhaps see a "pusher or thruster" making up to the judge and getting their exhibit so near that the judge almost falls over it. Do not be tempted to do the same thing, it does not help. Keep not too far away, but clear enough that the other dogs do not interfere with your exhibit, and if showing a dog, keep away from any of the bitches just in case you have a young Romeo on the end of the lead.

The judge will then make a decision and the steward will call out the awards. Let us say this is "your day out" and your dog is judged best of breed. You will be given another award card, and later if there is a competition for the best exhibit in the show which includes all the breeds competing you will be entitled to go into the big ring, when that old cry is again made: "All unbeaten dogs and bitches in the ring please". This time, of course, it means all the different top dogs in the breeds. And having embarked you on the final step towards the dizzy award of "best exhibit all breeds in show", I leave you to do the very best you can with a final tip. When taking up your place in the line, get among the other toy dogs, and do not stand against a Borzoi or a Great Dane, nor a snarling terrier. In this show game a pinch of common sense is worth five chapters of this book, even if you should remember them verbatim.

By the way, earlier in the book I gave you the names of the various Clubs fostering the breed; perhaps you have joined one or several of them. While waiting to compete in your breed, you might look at the catalogue and see if your Club is offering any special prizes confined to members. These may be Club Spoons which you can collect until you have a full set, or perhaps there is a cash offering. When you see there are specials offered; when the judging for best of breed has taken place, do not dash away, but stay near the table. You may not have actually won first, but if the winner is not a member of your club you can then step forward and tell the judge that you are a member and he will then mark you down in his book for the special prize. He will ask for your number, and do not simply say "I can't remember". Have the number pinned in its proper place or memorize it. While on this subject of numbers, when you have progressed somewhat you may decide to show three Pekes at the same show. You will then be given three numbers. Whatever you do, always ensure that you are wearing the correct number for the dog you are showing. So many exhibitors change their dog and not the number, and wrong awards are therefore marked in the judging book and cause endless trouble. I have known judges get so enraged by half-witted exhibitors that they have adopted the attitude, "You can't help me, then I don't help you", and another dog gets the award you might have had. Judges are only human. They are hard worked, often having to get a lot done in a limited time, and when you waste a judges' time it is also that of your fellow exhibitors, and the show promoters. Don't be a clot; keep on your toes, obey the rules, and you will be welcomed all along the line.

Immediately judging is over, do not rush up to the judge and ask silly questions, and remember that speaking to a judge during judging is not allowed. Make quite sure the judge has finished marking his awards, has thanked his stewards, and is taking a well-earned rest, then quietly ask if you may speak to him. You might even do it through a third party; one of the stewards. Make up your mind beforehand exactly what you wish to know, and when the judge listens to you, put your query concisely and be satisfied with your answer, and don't make his remarks a basis for a wandering dissertation on your troubles. There may be others waiting with their queries. Many a time will a foolish exhibitor go up to a judge, having failed to get an award, and ask "what is wrong with my dog?", and the judge, in reply, says, "it has a poor front", to be told "I know it has". Such people nearly drive one to distraction. And again, if you have won, do not go to the judge and ask what he thinks of your dog as so many do. Wait for the dog paper and see his report.

While on this subject of general ring-behaviour, before and after judging, always bear in mind that it is the dog the judge wishes to see and not yourself, however dolled up you may be for the occasion, so avoid getting between your dog and the judge.

I also warned you not to join the ranks of pugnacious exhibitors always pushing to the front. Equally, may I say don't be a retiring Jersey Lilly standing tucked away in a corner while the class is judged and the awards marked off, and then come out with the remark, "I have never been judged". If inadvertently you have been missed in a very crowded ring, before the judge has time even to pick up his book, go quietly up to the ring steward and say, "the judge has not seen this exhibit" and the steward will draw the judge's attention to you. Never go to the judge direct if there is a steward available.

A judge can re-judge a class if he chooses, but not one in ten will do it. A judge can also change his decision without having to give a reason, but few do so. One thing you may do after judging, which I think is quite gracious in a world where good manners are going by the board, is that when the judge happens to be free, and you have had a good win, walk up and say, "may I thank you for such a lovely day and I am delighted you like my dog". Or as a novice, you could say, "I am thrilled with the prize you gave me—it is the first I have ever won".

AN EYE TO THE SHOW RING

Nine times out of ten the judge will be delighted to know another new exhibitor has been successfully started, and will almost certainly offer you words of advice and encouragement. Don't be fussy—the judge has only done his job—but though the regular exhibitor may not think so, judges are really human and respond to a courteous acknowledgement of their efforts.

With knowledge acquired you may some time go to a show where you widely disagree with the judge. Even should you have the reddest of hair can I beg of you not to blackguard the judge. If you have to swallow your tonsils in an endeavour to keep your mouth shut for the time being, do so. Your remedy is never to show under that judge again, and what is more don't forget there are other qualified lookers-on who will be quick to resent the unfairness and take up the cudgels on your behalf. I can speak from actual experience of an incident when a great dog was beaten. The owner-handler, calm and dignified, took everything coming and quietly retired, but the ringsiders stood round, many with actual tears in their eyes, discussing the incident. Such things as these only do harm to one person, and that person is not the owner of the losing dog, provided one can retain one's dignity.

But to my mind there is one type even more poisonous than a bad-tempered loser, that is a boastful winner. It is, unless you are of a very stable temperament, quite a difficult thing to win gracefully. By this I do not mind, nor does anyone else, a spontaneous exhibition of pleasure, coupled with a 'hard lines' for the loser, but a boastful: "now which is the best in the breed, the show, the road or even the kennel", rubs people the wrong way and creates an adverse and lasting impression.

The award is only carrying the opinion of one judge for one day, and in any case one person saying your dog is great is better than your claiming greatness ten thousand times yourself. It has long been known that you can say what you like about a person, but you must not criticise his dog. It is one of the weaknesses of our make up and thus one can, with the passage of time, forgive a person going off the handle on a loss, deserved or otherwise, but no one forgives arrogance and boastfulness.

I have seen a youngster and even an oldster give a hop, skip and a jump with pleasure, on a win, in such a manner that everyone has looked on with an indulgent eye. Innate modesty may be overcome for the moment, but somehow it is still embodied in the demonstration and does not give offence. I am not suggesting that we can give a demonstration of cheerfulness on losing. Sometimes, especially where a wrong decision is concerned, the hurt can go too deep, but may I offer a very short motto to exhibitors—*win modestly and lose with dignity*.

One temptation I do ask you to resist and this is the natural one of after winning under a judge, to follow him or her from show to show for more wins. I know a number of people, who at Championship shows, will win only the once with any particular dog under the judge. At mixed shows I do not mean that you should miss an enjoyable fixture just because you have won under a breed judge, when at a later show there is just the odd class for you and you want to make further entries in variety classes. Common sense can be applied to this as to every other situation. Follow a judge if you wish, but take a different animal. You need not take your best dog twice running, but next time you may have a good puppy to bring out and then of course do not hesitate to enter under a judge who likes your type of animal. In this regard, when you have progressed to the time your kennel is getting known in the breed, the successful launching of a puppy is most important towards the success of his career. If you can get a good start under a first-class judge, you will find others will be inclined to take more notice of your puppy.

By degrees you will come to appreciate the better judges from the indifferent ones, and assess the value of your wins accordingly. There are judges in every breed whose award of a third to your dog will carry more weight than winning a first under another. Dog shows today are a costly business and no one blames you for entering with discretion. Beware the person who indirectly touts for entries. Be sure others have been approached, as you will find this type quite without conscience. If they should by hook or by crook get a decent entry, whatever they have said or hinted previously, you might well find yourself out of the prize money and in the position of suffering disappointment for your dog and rage against the judge.

If you have at all a sizeable Kennel there are bound to occur some animals who cannot achieve championship status, but yet are valuable assets as brood bitches for instance, or they may be good stud dogs, for it is not always the champion that begets the winners. These are very useful indeed when you feel you ought to give a judge a courtesy entry. Maybe the judge has done you very well at a previous show with firsts right through and lots of special prizes. They will appreciate your support at another show where you are not out to clear the board. These dogs, too, are very handy when you wish to support a new judge in the breed. You do not want to insult them by showing poor stuff, nor do you want, until a judge has proven himself, to allow him to practice on your prospective champion.

In all cases of the type I have just mentioned always pay the judge the compliment of presenting your dog in the very peak of condition and in the best coat possible. Handle it as carefully as you would in the open class at a championship show; in fact, I never advocate entering any show deliberately to lose, and with a 'don't care' attitude. The judge might resent this, and may think you consider yourself so important that you cannot possibly lose. Granted, you do not think this, but don't give others cause to think it, which is more to the point. I believe I can pick out people who have had a good education; I do not mean an expensive one, who have in their youth been in team competition more than individual competition. A type such as this, is, I think, helped in ring deportment. After a few shows you will find that the right type of people instinctively sort you out and take you, as it were, into the fold, sharing their simple pleasures at a show; the friendly offer at the lunch break, and little gestures. They appreciate that based on sound early education and team training you will not "let the side down" when it comes to competitive dog showing with all its very severe tests of character.

As I write this chapter there is an 'off stage' soft accompaniment of the words and music from the great hit of America *My Fair Lady* based on George Bernard Shaw's famous play *Pygmallion*, and I immediately think of Eliza Doolittle—with her agonies of "The rain in Spain stays mainly on the plain" and her battle with the aspirates. Lack of accent, and aitch trouble, did not affect her natural charm. When I refer to education I am not thinking of the type that gives superficial results. Natural gentility and gentleness will always get by with the more fortunate of your fellows, and I can sincerely say in a breed where we have a great many ladies and few men competing, that you will find, equally accepted and popular, people with the broadest of broad accents, and far from being endowed with worldly goods. Dog showing conducted at its highest level can be a most satisfying thing, so do not listen to subversive talk that judges are wrong or crooked and that your fellow exhibitors are for ever trying to steal a march on you. Don't misconstrue the efforts of another to win legitimately. It is up to you to do the same thing, profit by experience, and don't be too proud to profit by the experience of others. If your approach to dog showing is good and well meaning, then you will automatically meet and make friends with other good and well-meaning people. If you associate with those who dabble with tar you will be bound to get stained. You may think me too serious, too sentimental, too dictatorial, but believe me I am trying to advise you in your approach to your hobby; how to get the utmost enjoyment from it, and what is more, profitable enjoyment. That wise old saying still goes in this world, turned into doggy journalese, "what profit it a person who in winning a prize loses his soul" and what is equally important the respect of his fellows.

There is a type of exhibitor who will always damn a winning dog, always on the look-out for faults, and far from reticent in talking about them. Listen if you must, but do not, however tempting it may be to hear the dog which beat you damned, endorse that opinion in public or for that matter in private. The day may come when you are called in to judge and to write your report on the exhibits. Then without fear nor favour say what you think of the individual; why one dog went down, why another went up, and wherever practicable be constructive in your criticism.

The owl was credited with great wisdom because the more he saw the less he spoke, the less he spoke the more he heard, and we all might with great benefit to ourselves think on this old saying. Putting it another way, if you cannot say anything good about a person or a dog, then say nothing. You will automatically gain in popularity without actually seeking it; you will enjoy the actual show and reap double enjoyment when you put your feet up before your own fireside and think over the incidents of the day.

Many an article has been written on how to make dog showing pay. In previous sections I have tried to help you to make it pay financially, that dividends should take second place to the complete enjoyment of showing. After all, one has to live with oneself a major part of one's life, and it must be a good thing to so order one's public and competitive life that both can be equally satisfying.

9

SHOW ATTENDANCE

Previously I have explained how to get your dog used to company and trained to a lead so that you may be assured he will parade to advantage in the show ring. Between these two points is the matter of travel. With Pekingese the matter is superbly simple. Always travel them in boxes or baskets. If you have a car, take the dog around with you when on social jaunts. If not, spend some money on taking him on bus and train. You will find your dog invariably loves to travel, but if it is nervous this prior practice will pay untold dividends in settling him down to normal travelling so that he arrives at a show fairly calm and rested instead of a nervous, almost gibbering idiot.

Various aids for a poor traveller include giving the animal a good dose of powdered glucose, or a part of an anti-sea or air sick tablet. Others find of some use the very questionable trailing of a chain from the car to floor to discharge static electricity.

Of course, the best thing of all, in the rare event of your dog being a bad traveller, is to start an hour early, go leisurely through the veterinary inspection, let your dog quietly return to normal equilibrium then groom and bench him. Toys are specially privileged in that their box or basket may be put on top of normal wire benching, so long as there is a glass or wire front to enable the spectators to view the dog. They pay their money and expect to see the exhibits.

In this regard you must not have your dog off its bench or out of its basket for more than fifteen minutes unless it is actually competing in the ring. If you have a popular dog which has been plagued by too many spectators, instead of taking him to exercise for this period there is no harm in simply dropping the blind with which most show boxes are fitted, for a similar limited period. Failure to conform to this time limit when the dog is not legitimately on view may draw down on you a penalty from the Kennel Club if someone reports the dogs undue absence.

Your approach to the ring, your conduct and handling while actually competing and your attitude immediately after competing, have all been covered. Winning or losing, now comes the time to leave the show. In many cases if you come from over a prescribed distance you may be allowed to leave early. To gain this privilege some promoters insist that you apply at the time of making entries. Some allow you to go to the Secretaries' office, state your case, and if legitimate they will give you an early removal permit to leave the show. If you have won and fulfil this regulation you are safe to retain your wins and prize money. If you leave the show before the official closing time, without a permit and are reported for doing so, you run the risk of being fined and the cancellation of your prize money. Dog exhibitors are even more imaginative than the office boy on the day of a local cricket or football match in inventing excuses, the time-honoured one for the boy is grandmama's funeral.

I now realise I have stepped you out of the show without mentioning what are to me certain essential preliminaries I always carry ready mixed in correct proportions, "Dettol" and water. Before leaving the show, first turn over the blanket in the box on which the dog has been lying. Then rinse his mouth, sponge his stomach, frills and petticoats and soak his feet in the liquid. Dry him off and return him to his box, but never put him on the floor again or allow him to contact another dog. He, of course, will have been Epivaxed, together with most of your dogs at home, but you may have puppies about, and it would be asking for trouble if you did not properly disinfect the dog which has been in the ring in contact with so many others for so long a time. When you do arrive home, your own drill is, change your shoes before stepping over the border of your own kennel, and also thoroughly wash in "Dettol" and water. There are today, other more remote diseases against which inoculation does not create immunity. Therefore go through, without fail, this perhaps somewhat irksome drill. Wishing afterwards in a disaster is not much good.

10

FINAL NOTES FOR ESTABLISHED KENNELS

WITH a winning stud dog or two and several brood bitches, might I suggest you resist the temptation to let your kennel get out of hand. In other words never keep more dogs than you or your staff can successfully cope with. You may have a number of promising puppies. If you have not the room or cannot afford them, take your pick and, without qualm, let the others go. Believe me, your greatest advertisement for the kennel is to see puppies which win for others. It is a kennel club rule that in big shows the name of the dog, its sire, dam *and the Breeder* appear, so people attending a show, spotting a winner, immediately look for how it was bred and who bred it, and will automatically come to you to try and buy one as good. Otherwise there are the usual means of the specialist papers in which to advertise your stock and stud. With growing success your kennel may attract the attention of overseas buyers. You may have read or been told of wonderful sales and offers. Believe me, it is not every day a genuine offer of £10,000 for a dog is received. This was the price refused by Miss de Pledge and myself for Champion Ku Ku. Some may advertise that a magnificent sum has been refused, to enhance the chance of stud work for a dog, when in fact the offer has been made with no intention of it ever being accepted. Overseas buyers do pay well for our stock and so they should, for we have the finest Pekingese in the World. As I write, first, second, third and fourth winning Pekingese in the Hong Kong annual championship show were all exported by breeders in this country. What I want to say is, while demanding a full price, do not ask a fictitious one for an inferior dog. Better to lose a sale than have a dog go abroad to cause disappointment. In damaging your own reputation you also damage the standing of British dogdom as a whole. If you sell a dog at home or abroad at a bargain price, do not regret your loss of a few extra pounds, put that down to your advertising account, for you will be absolutely certain to receive repeat or additional orders. If you do sell for export., I would suggest you put the transaction in the hands of any of the several excellent organisations already established. They know the ropes—otherwise the regulations—they will take the responsibility from your shoulders, and all you have to do is to hand to them the dog in top form and then await that most satisfying of all cables "Dog arrived safely, absolutely delighted with him, thanks for selling him to me". If you have a heart at all, that is worth all sorts of pounds, shillings and pence.

In closing this short work on our beloved breed, as one great final motto, may I give you "keep the breed first and self-interest second", and you are bound to succeed.

11

PEDIGREES

BELOW will be found the pedigrees of some famous Pekingese which are portrayed in this book, and some of their major wins, illustrative of the heights which can be achieved by correct breeding.

CH: CAVERSHAM KU-KU of YAM K.C.S.B. 234-A.L.

BRED BY MISS CROWTHER AND OWNED BY MISS DE PLEDGE

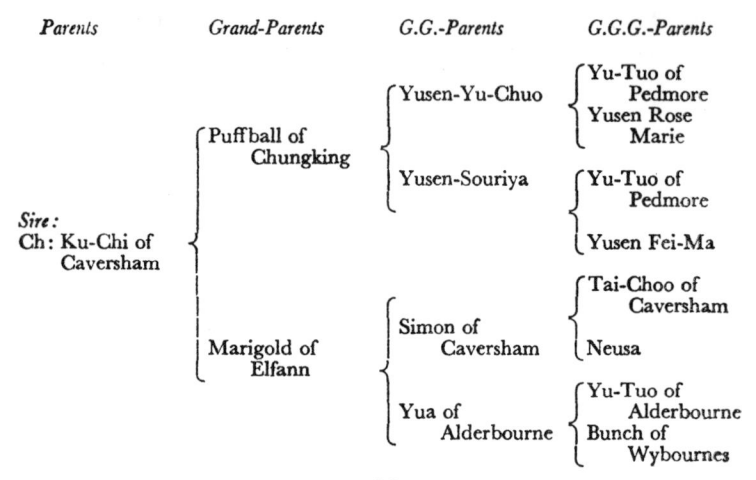

Parents	Grand-Parents	G.G.-Parents	G.G.G.-Parents
Sire: Ch: Ku-Chi of Caversham	Puffball of Chungking	Yusen-Yu-Chuo	Yu-Tuo of Pedmore / Yusen Rose Marie
		Yusen-Souriya	Yu-Tuo of Pedmore / Yusen Fei-Ma
	Marigold of Elfann	Simon of Caversham	Tai-Choo of Caversham / Neusa
		Yua of Alderbourne	Yu-Tuo of Alderbourne / Bunch of Wybournes

PEDIGREES

Parents	Grand-Parents	G.G.-Parents	G.G.G.-Parents
Dam: Regina of Yam	Ch: Tong-Tou of Alderbourne	Ch: Yu-Tong of Alderbourne	Puffball of Chungking / Yung-Bee of Alderbourne
		Panderh of Acol	Ching-Woo of Alderbourne / Angeline of Alderbourne
	Yu-Tu of Yam	Grey Toi of Alderbourne	Ch: Yusen-Yu-Toi / Young Bee of Alderbourne
		Wix Cherry	Kwai-Choo of Osbaston / Wix Stella

The winner up to date of thirty-nine certificates under thirty-nine different judges. Six times Best of All Breeds at Championship Shows.

CH: KU-CHI of CAVERSHAM, K.C.S.B. 419-A.D.

BRED BY MISS E. M. EVANS AND OWNED BY MRS. LUNHAM AND MISS DE PLEDGE

Parents	Grand-Parents	G.G.-Parents	G.G.G.-Parents
Sire: Puffball of Chungking	Yusen-Yu-Chuo	Yu-Tuo of Pedmore	Yu-Tuo of Alderbourne / Miss Tang of Alderbourne
		Yusen Rose Marie	Harmony of Mooda / Yusen-Fei-Ma
	Yusen-Souriya	Yu-Tuo of Pedmore	Yu-Tuo of Alderbourne / Miss Tang of Alderbourne
		Yusen-Fei-Ma	Yusen-Yu-Fei / Yusen-Wen-Dee

PEKINGESE

Parents	Grand-Parents	G.G.-Parents	G.G.G.-Parents
Dam: **Marigold of Elfann**	Simon of Caversham	Tai-Choo of Caversham	Yung-Tai-Choo of Caversham / Ch: Sha-Sha of Caversham
		Neusa	Pinky-Poo of Woodvale / Canton Wassums
	Yua of Alderbourne	Yu-Tuo of Alderbourne	Tai-Chaun of Alderbourne / Linnet
		Bunch of Wybournes	Ch: Yu-Fuh of Alderbourne / Deborah Pilese of Benckhampton

The Winner of thirty-two certificates under thirty-one different judges; twice in the last four Supreme Champions at Crufts; the sire of the great Champion Ku-Ku. Now deceased.

CH: TANG-YUA of ALDERBOURNE

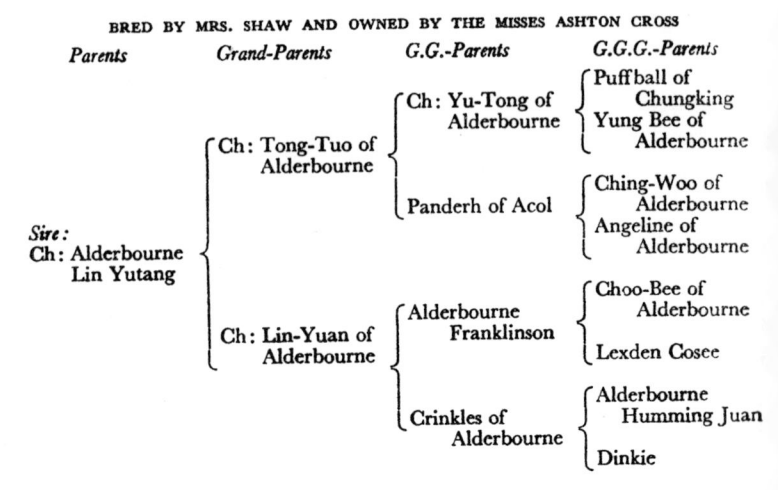

BRED BY MRS. SHAW AND OWNED BY THE MISSES ASHTON CROSS

Parents	Grand-Parents	G.G.-Parents	G.G.G.-Parents
Sire: **Ch: Alderbourne Lin Yutang**	Ch: Tong-Tuo of Alderbourne	Ch: Yu-Tong of Alderbourne	Puffball of Chungking / Yung Bee of Alderbourne
		Panderh of Acol	Ching-Woo of Alderbourne / Angeline of Alderbourne
	Ch: Lin-Yuan of Alderbourne	Alderbourne Franklinson	Choo-Bee of Alderbourne / Lexden Cosee
		Crinkles of Alderbourne	Alderbourne Humming Juan / Dinkie

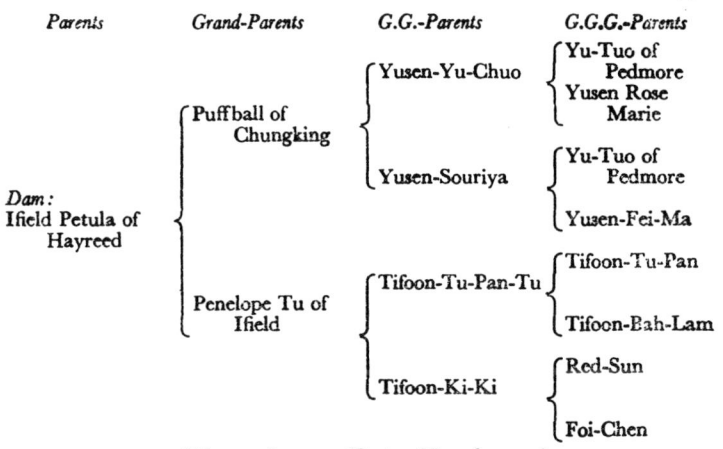

PEDIGREES

Parents	Grand-Parents	G.G.-Parents	G.G.G.-Parents
Dam: Ifield Petula of Hayreed	Puffball of Chungking	Yusen-Yu-Chuo	Yu-Tuo of Pedmore Yusen Rose Marie
		Yusen-Souriya	Yu-Tuo of Pedmore Yusen-Fei-Ma
	Penelope Tu of Ifield	Tifoon-Tu-Pan-Tu	Tifoon-Tu-Pan Tifoon-Bah-Lam
		Tifoon-Ki-Ki	Red-Sun Foi-Chen

Winner of ten certificates. Now deceased.

CHAMPION CHERYL OF CHINTOI, K.C.S.B. 188-A.V.

BRED AND OWNED BY MISS E. A. PAGE

Parents	Grand-Parents	G.G.-Parents	G.G.G.-Parents
Sire: Ch: Twee Choo of Caversham	Tu Choo of Caversham	Yung Tai Choo of Caversham	Tai-Choo of Caversham Zinnia of Caversham
		Tula of Aldercroft	Yusen Wang Hou Yusen Christina
	Kuela of Caversham	Ch: Ku-Chi of Caversham	Puffball of Chungking Marigold of Elfann
		Angela of Wykey	Ch: Yu-Tong of Alderbourne Miss Muffet of Wykey
Dam: Cherokee of Chintoi	Ch: Ku-Jin of Caversham	Ch: Caversham Ku-Ku of Yam	Ch: Ku-Chi of Caversham Regina of Yam
		Caversham Jin Jin of Wethersfield	Ku's Kin of Wethersfield D'Juli of Wethersfield
	Butterfly of Chintoi	Wei-Tsun of Chintoi	Che Sun Wei of Chintoi Tula of Chintoi
		Ming Tong of Chintoi	Ch: Yu-Tong of Alderbourne Bi-Jou of Chintoi

PEKINGESE

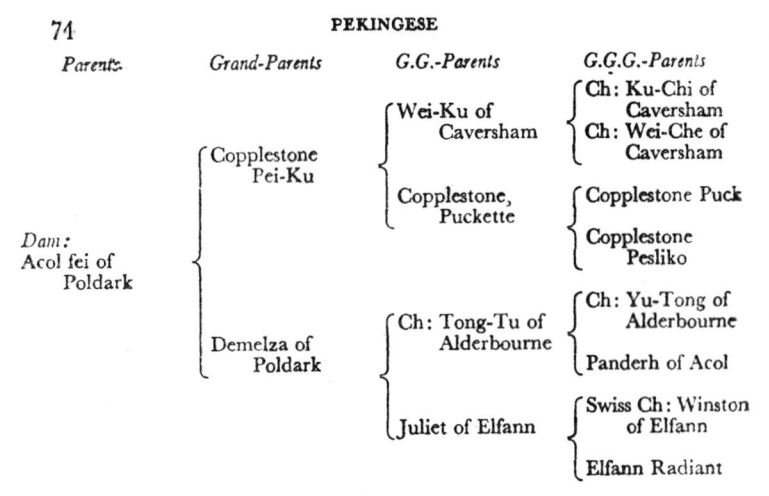

Parents	Grand-Parents	G.G.-Parents	G.G.G.-Parents
Dam: Acol fei of Poldark	Copplestone Pei-Ku	Wei-Ku of Caversham	Ch: Ku-Chi of Caversham Ch: Wei-Che of Caversham
		Copplestone, Puckette	Copplestone Puck Copplestone Pesliko
	Demelza of Poldark	Ch: Tong-Tu of Alderbourne	Ch: Yu-Tong of Alderbourne Panderh of Acol
		Juliet of Elfann	Swiss Ch: Winston of Elfann Elfann Radiant

Winner up to date of six certificates.

CHAMPION KU-JIN OF CAVERSHAM, K.C.S.B. 1611. A.P.

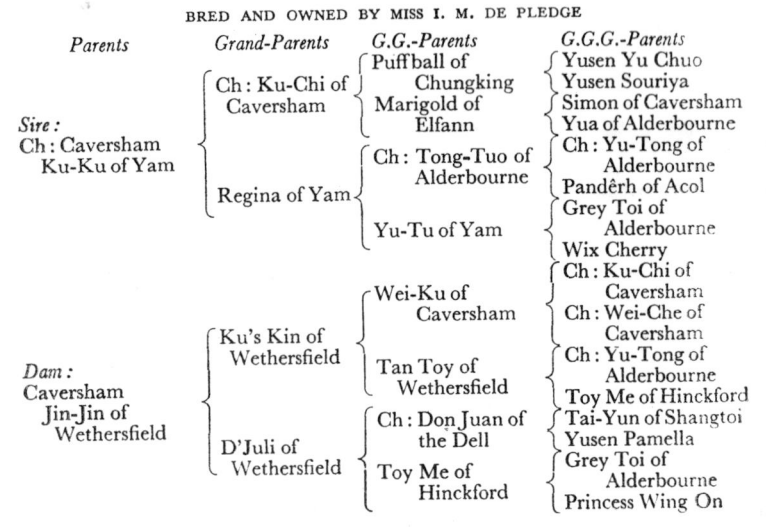

BRED AND OWNED BY MISS I. M. DE PLEDGE

Parents	Grand-Parents	G.G.-Parents	G.G.G.-Parents
Sire: Ch: Caversham Ku-Ku of Yam	Ch: Ku-Chi of Caversham	Puffball of Chungking	Yusen Yu Chuo Yusen Souriya
		Marigold of Elfann	Simon of Caversham Yua of Alderbourne
	Regina of Yam	Ch: Tong-Tuo of Alderbourne	Ch: Yu-Tong of Alderbourne Pandêrh of Acol
		Yu-Tu of Yam	Grey Toi of Alderbourne Wix Cherry
Dam: Caversham Jin-Jin of Wethersfield	Ku's Kin of Wethersfield	Wei-Ku of Caversham	Ch: Ku-Chi of Caversham Ch: Wei-Che of Caversham
		Tan Toy of Wethersfield	Ch: Yu-Tong of Alderbourne Toy Me of Hinckford
	D'Juli of Wethersfield	Ch: Don Juan of the Dell	Tai-Yun of Shangtoi Yusen Pamella
		Toy Me of Hinckford	Grey Toi of Alderbourne Princess Wing On

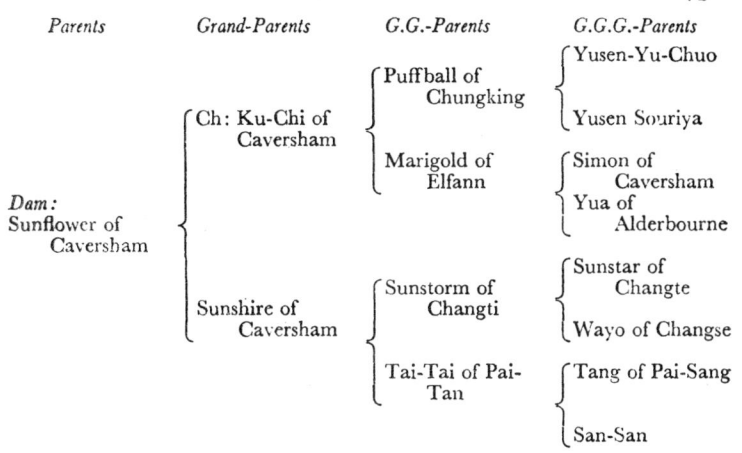

PEDIGREES

Parents	Grand-Parents	G.G.-Parents	G.G.G.-Parents
Dam: Sunflower of Caversham	Ch: Ku-Chi of Caversham	Puffball of Chungking	Yusen-Yu-Chuo
			Yusen Souriya
		Marigold of Elfann	Simon of Caversham
			Yua of Alderbourne
	Sunshire of Caversham	Sunstorm of Changti	Sunstar of Changte
			Wayo of Changse
		Tai-Tai of Pai-Tan	Tang of Pai-Sang
			San-San

Winner of seven certificates, up to date.

CH: KYRATOWN LU-TONG of REDSTOCK

BRED BY MISS RAINFORD AND OWNED BY MR. HINDLEY TAYLOR

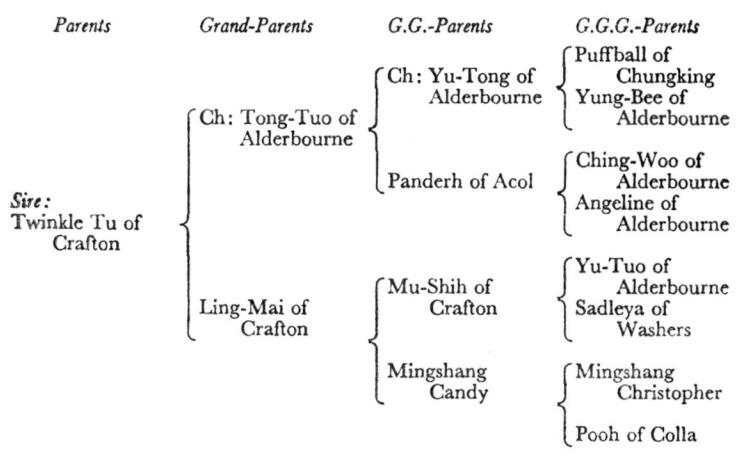

Parents	Grand-Parents	G.G.-Parents	G.G.G.-Parents
Sire: Twinkle Tu of Crafton	Ch: Tong-Tuo of Alderbourne	Ch: Yu-Tong of Alderbourne	Puffball of Chungking
			Yung-Bee of Alderbourne
		Panderh of Acol	Ching-Woo of Alderbourne
			Angeline of Alderbourne
	Ling-Mai of Crafton	Mu-Shih of Crafton	Yu-Tuo of Alderbourne
			Sadleya of Washers
		Mingshang Candy	Mingshang Christopher
			Pooh of Colla

Parents	Grand-Parents	G.G.-Parents	G.G.G.-Parents
Dam: Luminess of Redstock	Luminess of Moonland	Gold Model of Moonland	Buffy of Moonland Fo-Ming of Moonland
		Nedda of Moonland	Manlar of Moonland Chintz of Moonland
	Cont Ch: Redstock Ting-Choo of Liwood	Robin of Redstock	Tai-Choo of Caversham Too-Shoos of Redstock
		Choo-Li of Liwood	Tai-Choo Son of Caversham Glitter of Liwood

Winner of thirty-three certificates. Now retired.

APPENDIX I

BIBLIOGRAPHY

The Popular Pekingese by Dr. John Vlasto (Popular Dogs Publishing Co.)

The Book on Pekingese by Dorothy Slater (Wm. Nimmo).

The Pekingese by Mrs. Ashton Cross (A. Ouseley).

The Pekingese Handbook by Clifford L. B. Hubbard (Nicholson and Watson).

INDEX

AGENE 41
Argentum liquid 37
Assimilative calcium 26

BENBOWS DOG MIXTURE 45
Blanket bed 25
Bob Martin's powders 45
Bowels, looseness 47
Breeding 20
Breeding germs 33
Broken wrinkle 13

CALLEVA KENNELS 7-8
Canine hysteria 39-40
Cascara 37
Claws 36
Cleft palate 35-6
Collosal Argentum 37

DE PLEDGE, MISS 7, 26, 50, 68
'Dettol' 66
Diarrhoea 47

EAR CANKER 39
Ear carriage 13
'Epivax' 13, 20, 30
Exercise 16, 42
Exporting 68-9
Eye infections 15, 36, 38
,, irritation of 38
,, stomach 37
,, ulceration of 15, 36-7
Eyes 37

FEEDING 25, 40, 42-4
,, puppy 27
First season 20
Forceps 24
Foundation stock 13
Friars balsam 36

GROOMING 18, 19

HARD PAD 46
Honey 46
House Training 18
Hysteria 39-40

INGROWING LASHES 37
Indigestion 40

JUDGING 55-60

KARSWOOD DOG POWDERS 45
Kennel Club 49-51
Kennelling 15-17
,, bedding 16
,, cramping 16
Ku-Chi of Caversham 8
Ku-Ku of Yam 8, 68
'Kurmange' 45

LAXATIVES 37
Linseed oil 45
Liquid vermifuges 28

MATING 22-3
,, time of 23
Meat, raw 27-8, 30, 44

Mellanby, Professor 41
Milk, 27-8, 44
,, goats 27

PAPER TRAINING 18
Parish's Chemical Food 42
Pedigrees 70-6
Pekingese Clubs 21
'Pulvex' 45
Puppy, choosing a 30-1

REGISTRATION OF A PUPPY 49
Rickets 39 41, 43
Round worm 36
Rupture 37

SCISSORS 24
Shape of skull 13
Show attendance 65-7

Showing 46-64
,, exercising 52
,, feeding 52
,, handling 52
,, training 52
,, travelling 65
Skin trouble 45
Sleeve Pekes 11-12
Stud fees 33
Sulphur 45
Swann, Frank 40

VASELINE 36
Vlasto, Dr. 36

WARNER HILL, FRANK 39
Weaning 27-8
Worms 35-5